AUDIO MIXING
BOOT ★ CAMP

HANDS-ON BASIC TRAINING FOR MUSICIANS

Bobby Owsinski

Alfred Music Publishing Co., Inc.
P.O. Box 10003
Van Nuys, CA 91410-0003
alfred.com

ISBN-10: 0-7390-8239-6 (Book & DVD-ROM)
ISBN-13: 978-0-7390-8239-3 (Book & DVD-ROM)

Cover Photos
Mixing: © iStockphoto.com / Anthony Brown • Camouflage: © iStockphoto.com / Patrick Wong • Equipment: © Bobby Owsinski

 Alfred Cares. Contents printed on 100% recycled paper.

CONTENTS

CHAPTER 2

CHAPTER 3

CHAPTER 4

CHAPTER 5
PANNING

CHAPTER 6
COMPRESSION

CHAPTER 7

USING THE EQ

CHAPTER 8
ADDING REVERB 85

CHAPTER 9

ADDING DELAY

CHAPTER 10

MODULATION EFFECTS

PREFACE

WELCOME TO THE AUDIO MIXING BOOT CAMP. NOW, LISTEN UP, RECRUITS!

If you're reading this book, it's probably because you're either new to mixing and don't have the faintest idea what to do, or your mixes aren't anywhere near where you'd like them to be. I can help, but only if you're willing to put the time in and do the work because this is a different kind of book about audio mixing in that it's built around exercises.

Mixing is one of those things that you can't learn by reading, you have to learn by doing, and the more you do it, the better you become. The problem is that many new mixers just starting out don't know where to begin, and those that already know a little don't know what to do to get better. That's where I come in.

As your mixing drill sergeant, I'll take you through all the areas of mixing that will not only get you going on the right track, but possibly cut a lot of time off your learning curve. Rather than just covering the theory of mixing, you'll be pushing faders and moving knobs so that you'll learn the secrets of mixing faster and easier than you ever thought possible. Along the way I'll tell you the reasons behind the exercises as well as the specifics of what you're learning, but almost every topic in the book is strictly hands-on.

You still have to put in the work, but if you're into making your music sound better, you'll have a lot of fun along the way.

Hopefully you'll find the exercises enjoyable and each one to be a great learning experience. Sometimes an exercise may seem a bit off the wall at first, but be assured that it's there for you to learn why an action is seldom done in a mix. My goal is to teach you all the things that make a mix sound great, and everything you can do to make it sound bad as well. You may find you'll learn more from the later than the former.

Please note that I've included a number of examples on the DVD that you can learn from and play with, but feel free to use your own tracks if you have them.

Also note that this book won't cover basic theory or signal flow of a mixing console. Refer to your instruction manual, or a book like *The Mixing Engineer's Handbook* for more insight into this area. If fact, *The Mixing Engineer's Handbook* is also a great place to continue learning after you've finished this book, as it will give you a number of additional techniques that you can experiment with.

Okay, Recruit. Now hit the deck and give me 20, as we dig in deep into the world of mixing.

CHAPTER 1
MONITORING

Okay, listen up, recruits! It's time to get your barracks in order.

You can have the best monitoring chain that money can buy, but if it isn't set up correctly in your room, your mixes are going to be disappointing. On the other hand, even if you have inexpensive monitor speakers, you can get surprisingly good results if they're placed correctly in the room. That's why you have to tighten up your listening environment before you begin to mix.

The Listening Environment

Let's face it. Unless you're purpose-building your studio from the ground up, the majority of us overlooks our listening environment. Usually it's just the old "throw some speakers and a DAW up in an open corner of the room and go" routine where we try to get everything making sounds as quickly as possible and leave it at that. While it's possible that you can get lucky with a balanced sound and wide stereo field by just setting up a couple of nearfield monitors in your room without thinking much about it, usually that's not the case because normal garages, living rooms and bedrooms aren't intended as listening spaces and have little in the way of acoustic treatment. Whether you're treating your room or not (you really should - read my book *The Studio Builder's Handbook* for inexpensive ways to do it), the following steps are necessary to optimize what you're hearing.

The correct placement of the speakers is one of the most critical adjustments that you can make in improving the sound of your room. Before you do anything else, this place must be determined. Sometimes, even just a movement of a few inches backward or forward can make a big difference.

Determining The Listening Position

The first thing to do is to select the best place in the room for your listening position. The place that provides the best acoustic performance will almost always come from setting up lengthwise in the room because it's easier to avoid some of the problem room reflections (see Figure 1.1) that can plague the frequency response of the room. In other words, the speakers should be firing the long way down the room.

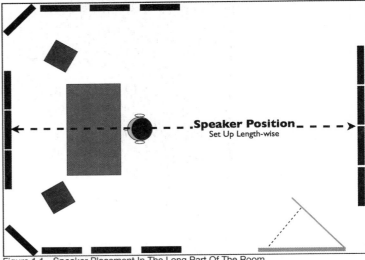
Figure 1.1 - Speaker Placement In The Long Part Of The Room

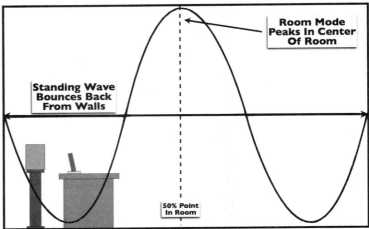
Figure 1.2: A Typical Standing Wave

Standing Waves

Without getting into too many technicalities, every room suffers from reflections that reinforce at the 50% point of the room, and diminish at the 25% and 75% points. That means that if you're listening position is exactly half-way in the room, one frequency will be extremely loud, but it might be non-existent at the 25% and 75% of the length of the room.

For example, in a typical room with a 12-foot length, the standing

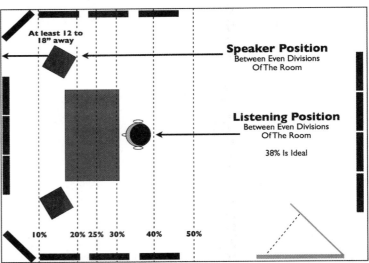
Figure 1.3: Placement In The Room

wave will be 47Hz (determined by the formula 1,130 ft. per sec. (the speed of sound)/12 feet x 2), which means that frequency will evenly bounce back and forth in the room. If you place either the speaker or the listening position mid-way in the room, or at the 50 percent point, 47Hz will reinforce and it will sound extremely loud. If you place the speakers or listening position at either a quarter of the way into the room (at the 25 percent point) or a quarter of the way from the rear wall (at the 75 percent point), 47Hz will cancel out (see Figure 1.2).

As a result, you want to place both the speakers and listening position somewhere in between 25, 50 and 75 percent of the room (30, 40, 60 and 80 percent are good to stay away from as well), and place the speakers and listening area at an odd non-divisible number like 27, 38, 45 percent etc. (see Figure 1.3). Although these placement points will get you in the ballpark, prepare to move everything a few inches forward or backward even after you've placed everything.

The 38 percent point in the room may or may not be the right place for speaker placement in your particular room, which is why you must be prepared to experiment with placement a few inches backward or forward once all of the treatment is in place. There are so many variables involved with just about any room that even the best designers with the best equipment can't even precisely predict the correct placement, and as a result, may spend an entire week just tweaking the speaker and listening positions, so don't be surprised if it takes some time and experimentation to get this right.

While these numbers may be all well and good, they don't help you much if you don't have that much space to play with. If that's the case, the following quick fixes can still make a considerable difference.

Acoustic Quick Fixes

Without having to acoustically treat your room (which should always come first if you can), here are a few simple things that you can do to instantly improve the performance of your playback system.

- **Avoid placing the speakers up against a wall.** This usually results in some strong peaks in the low-frequency response. The further away you can get from the wall, the less it influences the frequency response of your monitors and the smoother that response will be. Figure an absolute minimum of twelve inches, although more is better, as long as you stay out of the 25% point of the room as mentioned above.

- **Avoid the corners of the room.** Even more severe than the wall is a corner, since it will reinforce the low end even more than a speaker placed against a wall. The worst case is if only one speaker is in the corner. This will cause the response of your system to be lopsided on the low-end towards the speaker located there.

- **Avoid being closer to one wall of the room than the other.** If one speaker is closer to one side wall than the other, once again you'll get a totally different frequency response between the two because of phase and reflection issues. It's best to set up directly in the center of the room if possible. Symmetry is essential to keep a balanced stereo image with a stable frequency response in the room. That means that your sweet spot will be in the exact center of the room if the speakers are exactly the same distance from each side wall. While it may seem tempting to set up some other way, acoustically you could be asking for trouble.

- **Avoid different types of wall absorption.** If one side of the room contains a window and the other is drywall, carpet or acoustic foam, once again you'll have an unbalanced stereo image because one side will be brighter sounding than the other. Try to make the walls on each side of the speakers the same material.

- **Make sure you place the speakers on stands.** Speakers mounted directly on a desk or console will defeat the purpose of much of the acoustic treatment. Mark the position of the speakers with masking tape, and mark the position in one-inch increments up to six inches either way from the wall so you don't have to re-measure in the event that you have to move things. Exact distances are critical, so always use a tape measure because even an inch can make a big difference in the sound.

Exercise Pod - Improving The Listening Environment

E1.1: Play a song that you think sounds great and you're very familiar with. Place your monitors at the 25% point of your room. Does the frequency response change? Are some bass frequencies missing? What happened to the stereo image? Are some bass frequencies reinforced?

E1.2: A) Move the speakers a few inches backwards from the 25% point. Does the frequency response change? Are some bass frequencies missing? Are some bass frequencies reinforced? Is the response smoother?

B) Move the speakers a few inches forwards from the 25% point. Does the frequency response change? Are some bass frequencies missing? What happened to the stereo image? Are some bass frequencies reinforced? Is the response smoother?

E1.3: Now move the speakers so they're only a few inches away from the front wall. Does the frequency response change? Are some bass frequencies missing? What happened to the stereo image? Are some bass frequencies reinforced? Is the response smoother?

E1.4: Place one speaker in a corner of the room. Does the frequency response change? Are some bass frequencies missing? Are some bass frequencies reinforced? Is the response smoother?

E1.5: A) If your speaker setup is not placed in the exact center of the room, make a mental note as to how it sounds.

B) Now move the speakers to the exact center of the room between the walls. Does the frequency response change? What happened to the stereo image? Are some bass frequencies missing? Are some bass frequencies reinforced? Is the response smoother?

Basic Monitor Setup

Now that your listening position is placed correctly in the room, it's time to set up your monitors. While most home studios seem to have a random amount of space between their monitors, there are a number of general guidelines you can use to optimize your setup. Since most rooms are unique in some way in terms of dimensions or absorbent qualities, you may have to vary from the following outline a little, but these are good places to start from.

- **Check The Distance Between The Monitors.** If the monitors are too close together, the stereo field will lack definition. If the monitors are too far apart, the focal point or "sweet spot" will be too far behind your head and you'll hear the left or the right side individually, but not both together as one. The rule of thumb is that the speakers should be as far apart as their distance from the listening position. That is, if your listening position is 4 feet away from the monitors, then start by moving them 4 feet apart so that you make an equilateral triangle between you and the two monitors. (Figure 1.4).

- That being said, it's been found that 67 ½ inches from tweeter to tweeter seems to be an optimum distance between speakers, because it focuses the speakers three to six inches behind your head (which is exactly what you want).

- **Check The Angle Of The Monitors.** Not angling the speakers properly will cause smearing of the stereo field, which is a major cause of a lack of instrument definition when you're listening to your mix. The correct angle is somewhat determined by taste, as some mixers prefer the monitors angled directly at their mixing position while others prefer the focal point (the point where the sound from the tweeters converges) anywhere from three to 24 inches behind them to widen the stereo field (see Figure 1.5).

- It's been found over time that an angle of 30 degrees that's focused about 18 inches behind the mixer's head works the best in most cases.

- A great trick for finding the correct angle is to mount a mirror over each tweeter and adjust the speakers so that your face is clearly seen in both mirrors at the same time when you are in your mixing position.

- **Check How The Monitors Are Mounted.** If at all possible, it's best to mount your monitor speakers on stands just directly behind the meter bridge of the console or edge of your desk. This gives you a much smoother frequency response.

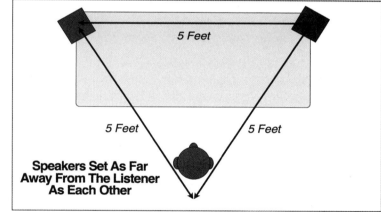

Figure 1.4 Speakers And Listener In An Equilateral Triangle

- Monitors that are placed directly on top of a computer desk or console meter bridge without using any isolation are subject to low-frequency cancellations because the sound travels through the desk or console, through the floor and reaches your ears before the direct sound from the monitors through the air gets there. This causes some frequency cancellation and a general smearing effect of the audio. If you must set your speakers on the desk or console, place them on a 1/2 or 3/4 inch piece of open cell neoprene, a thick mouse pad or two, or something like the Primacoustic Recoil Stabilizers (see Figure 1.6). You'll be surprised how much better they sound as a result.

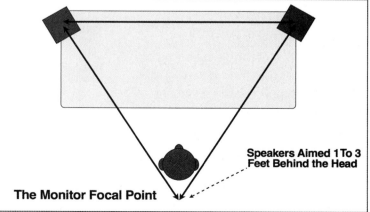

Figure 1.5 The Monitor Focal Point

• **Check How The Monitor Parameters Are Set.** Almost everyone uses powered monitors these days, but don't forget that many have a few parameter controls either on the front or rear. Be sure that these are set correctly for the application (make sure you read the manual) and are set the same on each monitor.

• **Check The Position Of The Tweeters.** Many monitors are meant to be used in an upright position, yet users frequently will lay them down on their sides. That makes them easier to see over, but the frequency response suffers as a result. That being said, if the speakers are designed to lay on their sides, most mixers prefer that the tweeters be on the outside towards the walls because the stereo field is widened (see Figure 1.7). Sometimes tweeters to the inside works but that usually results in the stereo image smearing. Try it both ways and see which one works best for your application.

• If your speakers are placed upright, be sure that the tweeters are head-height since the high frequency response at the mixer's position will suffer if they're too high and firing over your head. Sometimes it's necessary to even flip them over and place them on their tops in order to get the proper tweeter height.

Exercise Pod - Speaker Placement

E1.6: Play a song that you think sounds great and you're very familiar with.

A) Place the monitors exactly 67 1/2 inches apart. What does the stereo image sound like? What happens to the frequency balance of the speakers?

B) Now move the speakers closer together. What happens to the stereo image? What happens to the frequency balance of the speakers?

C) Now move the speakers further apart beyond the 67 1/2 inches. What happens to the stereo image? What happens to the frequency balance of the speakers?

E1.7: A) Angle the monitors so that they are pointing directly at the center of your head. What is the stereo image like?

B) Now angle the monitors so that they're aiming at a point about six inches behind your head. What is the stereo image like now?

E1.8: A) If your monitors are sitting on your desk or console, place a mouse pad or two underneath each

Figure 1.6 Yamaha NS-10's On Primacoustic Recoil Stabilizers

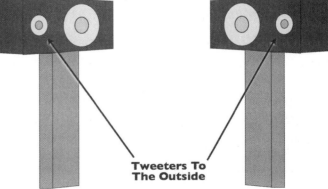

Tweeters To The Outside

Figure 1.7 Speakers With Tweeters To The Outside

one. What does it sound like? Did the low end get tighter and more focused? What's the stereo field like?

B) Place the speakers back on the console or desk, but without the mouse pads. Does it sound any different? What's the stereo field like?

C) If you have stands, now place them back on the stands. Does it sound any different? What's the stereo field like?

E1.9: A) If your monitor speakers have parameter controls on the back, randomly change the controls on the right speaker. What happens to the frequency response? What happens with the stereo image?

B) Now set the parameter controls so that they're exactly the same on each speaker (including the volume control if there is one). What happens to the stereo image? What happens to the low-end frequency response?

E1.10: A) Lay each speaker down on its side so that the tweeters are positioned toward the wall. What happens to the stereo image? What happens to the frequency response?

B) Now flip each speaker so that the tweeters are positioned on the inside towards each other. What happens to the stereo image? What happens to the frequency response?

How To Listen

We've been listening to the world around us all of our lives without thinking about it, but when it comes to mixing, we must take our listening ability to another level altogether. The following explanations and exercises are designed to make you think about what you're listening to while mixing, as well as to provide you with a set of tools to make sure that your mix translates well to all listening environments.

Basic Listening Technique

It's time to develop your critical listening skills. All of your life you've been listening to things as a whole. When you were outside in the park, you heard the dogs barking, birds chirping, a police car siren in the distance, children laughing while they were playing; but you mostly heard it all as one sound and only occasionally zeroed in on a portion of it without realizing it. When you went to a party, you heard the music in the background, guests laughing and talking, ice cubes tinkling in the glass as drinks were being made, and your ears might've picked up a conversation in the distance with a tidbit of juicy gossip. That was the beginning of critical listening. When you listened to a song on the radio, you listened to the song as a whole, and never really listened to the individual parts of the mix, unless you heard a particular instrument that you played.

Now it's time to begin to break those sound sculptures down into individual parts. This means identifying individual musical instruments, mix elements, frequency response, mix balance, and ambience, to name a few. Beware, after you begin to do this, you'll never hear music in the same way again, for better or worse.

Exercise Pod - What To Listen For

Play back one of your favorite songs, but make sure it's available at the highest resolution possible, which means CD, vinyl, or if it's one of your mixes, directly from your DAW. You're going to learn to listen to this mix in a different way.

E1.11: Listen to the mix. How many individual instruments can you identify?

E1.12: Listen to the mix. What part of the frequency spectrum does each instrument or vocal take up?

E1.13: Listen to the mix. How many different types of ambience (natural or artificial reverb) can you identify? Does each instrument have its own ambience? Is there one general ambience that pulls everything together? Does anything have a noticeable delay?

E1.14: Listen to the mix. What is the most interesting thing in the mix? Is it a vocal or an instrument or a sound effect? Is there an effect that catches your ear?

E1.15: Listen to the mix. What is the frequency balance of the mix as a whole like? Are there a lot of high frequencies? Does the song have a deep bottom end?

E1.16: Listen to the mix. Does the song have a lot of dynamics? Does it seemed to be compressed? Can you hear the compression on individual instruments or vocals?

How Loud (Or Soft) Should I Listen?

One of the greatest misconceptions about music mixers (especially the great ones) is that they mix at high volume levels. Some do, and at excruciatingly loud levels as well, but most mixers find that they get better balances that translate well to the real listening world by monitoring at conversation level (79 dB SPL) or even lower.

High SPL levels for long periods of time are generally not recommended for the following reasons:

1) Exposure to high volume levels over long periods of time my cause long-term physical damage.

2) High volume levels for long periods of time will not only cause the onset of ear fatigue, but physical fatigue as well. This means that you might effectively only be able to work six hours instead of the normal eight (or 10 or 12) that are possible if listening at lower levels.

3) The ear has different frequency response curves at high volume levels that overcompensate on both the high and low frequencies. This means that your high-volume mix will generally sound pretty limp when it's played at softer levels.

4) Balances tend to blur at higher levels. What sounds great at higher levels won't necessarily sound that way when played softer. However, balances that are made at softer levels always work when played louder.

Now this isn't to say that all mixing should be done at the same level and everything should be played quietly. In fact, music mixers (as opposed to film mixing, which always uses one constant level) tend to work at a variety of levels: loud for a minute to check the low end, and moderate while checking the EQ and effects. But the final balances usually will be done quietly.

Sometimes, the only way that you can check how much low-end is on a mix is to turn it up to a moderately loud level for a brief period, so don't be afraid to do that if needed. Just remember that keeping it up loud for long periods of time probably won't help your mix translate to other systems too well.

Exercise Pod - Listening Levels

E1.17: Set up one of the example mixes from the DVD supplied with this book.

Listen to the mix at low level, then turn it up to medium and then very loud levels. Can you hear the frequency response changing as the volume changes? Is there more or less high end? Is there more or less low end?

E1.18: Listen to the mix at a very low, barely perceptible level.

A) Increase the level of the kick drum by 2 dB. Can you hear the balance of the song change? Does the kick drum seem louder?

B) Return the kick drum to its original level. Now increase the level of the bass by 2 dB. Can you hear the balance of the song change? Does the bass seem louder?

C) If you can't hear the difference at 2 dB, at what level can you hear it?

E1.19: Now turn the level of the mix up to a level that's slightly louder that comfortable.

A) Increase the level of the kick drum by 2 dB. Can you hear the balance of the song change? Does the kick drum seem louder?

B) Return the kick drum to its original level. Now increase the level of the bass by 2 dB. Can you hear the balance of the song change? Does the bass seem louder?

C) If you can't hear the difference at 2 dB, at what level can you hear it?

E1.20: Listen to your mix at a very low, barely perceptible level.

A) Raise the level of the lead vocal by 2 dB. Can you hear the balance of the song change? Does the vocal seem louder?

B) Return the lead vocal to its original level. Now increase the level of the rhythm guitar by 2 dB. Can you hear the balance of the song change? Does the guitar seem louder?

C) If you can't hear the difference at 2 dB, at what level can you hear it?

E1.21: Now turn the level of the mix up to a level that's slightly louder that comfortable.

A) Increase the level of the lead vocal by 2 dB. Can you hear the balance of the song change? Does the vocal seem louder?

B) Return the lead vocal to its original level. Now increase the level of the rhythm guitar by 2 dB. Can you hear the balance of the song change? Does the guitar seem louder?

C) If you can't hear the difference at 2 dB, at what level can you hear it?

Listening On Several Speaker Systems

If you don't have an alternate monitor system yet, then what are you waiting for? Most veteran mixers use at least a couple of systems to get a feel for how everything sounds — the main system where the mixer does all of the major listening work, and an alternate system for a different perspective.

The alternate speaker is used simply as a balance check to make sure that one of the instruments isn't either too loud or too soft in the mix. Also, one of the arts of mix balance is getting the kick drum and bass guitar to speak well on a small system, which is why an alternative monitor system is so important.

The second set of monitors doesn't have to be great. In fact, the crappier they are, the better. Even a set of ten dollar computer speakers can do. The idea is to have a second set that will give you an idea of what things sound like in that world, since unfortunately, there are a lot more people listening on crappy monitors than good ones these days.

Exercise Pod - Listening On Multiple Monitors

E1.22: Listen to a mix on your normal monitors, then switch to your alternate monitors (make sure they're at exactly the same level). Is the frequency response different? Is the balance different? Is the low end different? Can you hear the bass better, or does it disappear? Can you hear the kick drum better, or does it disappear?

Listening In Mono

Sooner or later your mix will be played back in mono somewhere along the line, so it's best to check what will happen before you're surprised later. Listening in mono is a time-tested operation that gives the mixer the ability to check phase coherency and balances. Let's look at each one individually.

Phase Coherency

When a stereo mix is combined into mono, any elements that are out of phase will drop in level or even completely cancel out. This could be because the left and right inputs to the speakers are wired out of phase (pin 2 and pin 3 of the XLR connector are reversed) which is the worst-case scenario. Another possibility is that a cable was similarly out of phase when recording, or perhaps a phase switch was inadvertently selected during recording or mixing. Regardless of how it happened, an out-of-phase effect can cause the lead vocal or solo to cancel out and disappear from the mix, which certainly isn't something that you want to have happen. As a result, it's prudent to listen in mono once in a while just to make sure that a mono disaster isn't lurking in the wings.

Balances

Many engineers listen to their mix in mono strictly to balance elements together since they feel that they hear the balance better this way. Listening in mono is also a great way to tell when an element is masking another. As legendary engineer Andy Johns (Led Zeppelin, the Rolling Stones, Van Halen, Eric Clapton) once told me, "That used to be the big test (mixing in mono). It was harder to do and you had to be a bloody expert to make it work. In the old days we did mono mixes first then did a quick one for stereo. We'd spend 8 hours on the mono mix and half an hour on the stereo."

Exercise Pod - Listening In Mono

E1.23: If there is a mono switch on your console or DAW, select it to listen to the mix in mono. Have any instruments, vocals or reverb disappeared from the mix?

E1.24: Listen to the mix in mono. Are there any instruments that are fighting or covering up another instrument or vocal?

E1.25: Listen to the mix in mono. Raise the level, walk out of the room and listen from afar. Does the mix still hold together or does one instrument, vocal or frequency stand out?

CHAPTER 2
SESSION SETUP

There's a good argument to be made that the setup for a mix session is almost as critical as the mix itself. Proper setup allows you to get into the right headspace to hear what you need to hear over long periods of time. It helps your efficiency during the mix when you know the session is properly labeled and all the assignments, effects and routing are preset beforehand. Once you get into the flow of things, you don't ever want to stop for something technical that could've been taken care of a lot earlier.

We can break session setup down into two elements: prepping your mix and prepping yourself. Let's look at each.

Prepping Your Mix

This is where you get everything in your session prepped for the mix by making things easy to find. You may have to tweak things as you go along, but it will take you far less time as a result of this process, which will keep you in the creative flow of your mix.

Make A Session File Copy

Before you do anything else, make a copy of the session that's designated as the "mix" and name it something descriptive like "songtitle mix" so it's easy to locate (see Figure 2.1). This also keeps your previous session safe if you ever have to go back to it.

I personally always put a date in the file name, but that's not necessary since most of the time it's built into the meta data and can be easily determined by looking at the file info.

▼ 📁 Do What We Want– Village	Today, 12:58 PM
▶ 📁 Audio Files	Nov 27, 2009, 9:32 PM
ⓐ Do What We Want 12-15-9dec.ptf	Dec 15, 2009, 1:23 PM
ⓐ Do What We Want TV 4-9-10.ptf	Apr 9, 2010, 8:17 PM
ⓐ Do What We Want TV mix 4-9-10a.ptf	Apr 9, 2010, 9:27 PM
▶ 📁 Exports	Dec 14, 2009, 12:17 PM
▶ 📁 Fade Files	Oct 17, 2010, 12:38 PM
▶ 📁 old	Dec 15, 2009, 1:23 PM

Figure 2.1: A Descriptive File Title

It's not uncommon to have multiple versions of the same session during the same day, so I like to differentiate one from another with letters of the alphabet at the end of the title, like "rosegarden mix 9-9-11a," "rosegarden mix 9-9-11b" and so on.

If you are able, color code the file as well so it's easier to identify. I like to start with a series of colors that show the stage of completion. Like a traffic light, I'll start with red for "stop" and end with green for "go" or finished, but obviously use whatever colors work for you.

While you're at it, make a copy of the session file on another hard drive, flash drive, online backup, or any place that you can easily grab it if for some reason you find the file you're working on is suddenly corrupted.

Arrange Your Tracks

Deleting or hiding tracks that won't be used and ordering the tracks that will be used may be the single most useful thing you can do while prepping your mix. Here's what to do.

Delete Empty Tracks

Any empty tracks take up space in your edit and mix windows without adding anything useful, so it's best to delete them. During tracking or overdubs, it frequently makes sense to have empty tracks readily available, but if you've gotten to the mix without using them, you know they probably won't be needed. Delete them.

Deactivate And Hide Unused Tracks

Any tracks that you know won't be used just soak up your computer's system resources. Even if you have a power machine, these resources may become a precious quantity if you end up using a lot of plug-ins during the mix. Deactivate them, then hide them from the timeline and mix panels so they don't distract you.

Reorder Your Tracks

This isn't absolutely necessary, but it does make tracks easier to find during the mix. The idea is to group any similar instruments or vocals together, so all the guitars are next to each other, the drums and percussion next to one another, and all the vocals are together.

Color-Code The Tracks

Once again this isn't absolutely necessary, but it sure does make things easier to find if your DAW app has this ability. For instance, all the drums might be red, guitars blue, the vocals yellow, and so on.

Correctly Label The Tracks

Many workstation apps automatically assign a name to any new track that has been recorded, but unfortunately they usually don't relate to the instrument. It's really easy to mistake one track for another and turn a fader or parameter knob up and up and wonder why nothing is happening, only to find that you're tweaking the wrong track. That's why it's important to clearly label each track. You'll

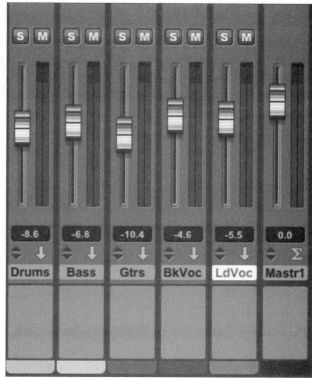

Figure 2.2: Setting Up Subgroups

be happy with yourself later if you re-label a track with a name like "gt166," to something like "guitar" or "gtr."

Insert Section Markers

Markers are truly one of the big time savers in any DAW, and if you haven't done so already, now is the time to do it. Most veteran mixers insert a marker a bar or two before each new section, and also make sure that other points like drum fills, accents or even the half-way point in a section are marked as well.

Set Up Subgroups

Sub-groups are extremely useful during mixing because they allow you to group similar elements of the mix so you can make adjustment by instrument sections, rather than individually (see Figure 2.2). Your mix will go a lot faster if your set up the subgroups and assign the particular channels to them ahead of time.

Typical groups might be drums, guitars (if there's more than one or they're in stereo), lead vocals (if there's a double), background vocals, horns, strings and synths.

Set Up Your Effects

Most mixers have a standard set of effects that they set up before they mix. We'll cover this more in Chapters 8 and 9, but one setup that works well even for tracking and overdubs is:

For Drums: A reverb using a dark room set to about 1.5 seconds of decay with a pre-delay of 20 milliseconds.

For All Other Instruments: A plate with about 1.8 seconds of decay and a pre-delay of 20 milliseconds.

For Vocals: A delay of about 220 milliseconds.

It's amazing how well these settings work without any tweaking. Another common setup is two reverbs and two delays, setup as follows:

Short Reverb: A room program with the decay set from .5 to 1.5 seconds of decay with a short pre-delay timed to the track.

Long Reverb: A plate or hall program with a decay set from 1.5 to 4 seconds of decay and a pre-delay of as little as 0 or as much as 150 ms timed to the track (depends on your taste and what's right for the song).

Short Delay: A delay of about 50 to 200 milliseconds.

Long Delay: A delay from about 200 to 400 or milliseconds.

Your own particular starting point might use a lot more effects, or you may prefer to

add effects as needed during the mix. Regardless, it's a good idea to have at least some effects set up before you start the mix so you won't break your concentration to set them up later. We'll look at some other effects setups later in Chapters 8 and 9.

Assign The Channels

Usually you know ahead of time that there are certain tracks that will use a certain effect (like the drums or snare to a short reverb). It's best to assign those channels to the appropriate sends and pan them accordingly before your mix begins.

Insert Compressors And Limiters

Chances are that at least a few channels, like the kick, snare, bass and vocal, will need a compressor during the mix. That's why it's a good idea to insert the compressor ahead of time during mix prep. Just remember to leave it bypassed

Figure 2.3: A Fully Prepped Mix

until you decide you need it (see Figure 2.3). We'll discuss compressors and limiters more in Chapter 6.

Exercise Pod - Prepping Your Mix

E2.1: A) Make a copy of the session file. Rename it and assign it a color. Can you easily find it in a group of files?

B) Make a second copy of the session file on another hard drive, flash drive, or online backup as a safety.

E2.2: Arrange your tracks.

A) Delete empty tracks.

B) Deactivate and hide unused tracks.

C) Reorder the tracks by instrument or vocal kind.

D) Color code the tracks in logical groups.

E) Rename the tracks so that they're easy to find.

E2.3: Go through the song and add markers right before the beginning of every section. Can you easily find them?

E2.4: Set up and assign sub-groups to anything with multiple tracks like drums, guitars, and vocals.

E2.5: A) Add four effects channels.

B) Insert two reverbs and two delays on them.

C) Assign them to the stereo buss.

D) Assign the sends to the effects to the appropriate channels.

E2.6: Insert compressors on the kick drum, snare drum, bass, and lead vocals. Keep them bypassed.

Prepping Yourself

Now that the technical portion of the mix is set up, it's time to get yourself prepared to mix. Each mix requires focus and concentration, and this is where we get ourselves into the proper headspace.

Play Something You Know

The most important thing during your own personal prep time is to play at least one song or mix that you know well, so you have a reference point as to what the room and monitors sound like. Listening to a mix or two will also calibrate your ears to the listening environment, which will help to keep you from over- or under-EQing as you go along.

Take Notes

During the course of a long mix you'll probably have to take some notes, so have a pen and a pad of paper, or even some Post-it notes, ready to write on. If you're using a hardware controller, you'll need a roll of console tape. Permacel P-724 is the type that can be reapplied without leaving any sticky residue behind to mark the names of the channels.

Make Yourself Comfortable

Most mixes take a while, so you need to be comfortable. Make sure your clothes and shoes are comfy, the room temperature is just right, and the lighting is adjusted so you can easily see any monitor screens that you may be using. It's also a good idea to have some beverages and a snack ready for later when you need a break.

Setting up for a mix is a lot more work that you might have thought, but it's time put to good use. Once these things are out of the way, your files, tracks, mind and ears are all set for the mix ahead.

Exercise Pod - Prepping Yourself

E2.7: A) Play a song or mix that you know well at a medium comfortable volume.

B) Play the same song or mix at a very loud volume. Is the frequency response any different?

C) Play the same song or mix at a very low volume. Is the frequency response any different?

E2.8: A) Have plenty of pens and blank paper available.

B) Apply console tape and name the tracks if you're using a console or controller

E2.9: A) Make sure your shoes and clothing are comfortable.

B) Make sure the room temperature is comfortable.

C) Make sure that refreshments are available.

CHAPTER 3
MIXING BASICS

There are many great mixers that can't tell you exactly what they do because they do it entirely by feel, intuition and experience. These qualities are usually developed over a long period of time with a lot of experimentation thrown in. You want to get there faster than that, which is why you're reading this book, so a more structured method of learning about mixing is required. Before you start moving faders, it's important to understand why you're doing it, and what you're listening for first.

A Brief History

Before we cover the mechanics of mixing, it's important to understand how this art has developed over the years.

In the early days of recording in the 1950s, mixing certainly was far from how we know it today, since the recording medium was mono and a big recording date used only 4 microphones. With the development of tape machines with more and more tracks, larger mixing consoles with more and more channels were required as well. Soon consoles were so large that they needed computer automation and recall in order to adequately manage these larger track and channel counts. What we consider "mixing" evolved from a simple balancing of a few microphones fed into one or two tracks with very few outboard tools available, into a highly creative process managing more than a hundred tracks and channels with racks and racks of outboard gear. This required that the mixer develop not only a new approach to mixing, but a whole new way of listening as well.

Once tape machines were capable of more audio tracks, two major transformations occurred.

Recording changed from capturing a performance of many musicians and vocalists in the studio, to creatively molding a song through overdubs. For instance, most of the hit songs of the 1950s and early '60s (like anything from The Beatles, RCA Records in Nashville, Motown Records or Phil Spector) were recorded with virtually all the musicians playing in the room at the same time. The overdubs

Figure 3.1: An MCI 24 Track Tape Machine

consisted of vocals (lead and background at the same time), maybe horns or strings, and occasionally another lead instrument. From the 1970s onward when the 16-track, and later 24-track, tape machines came into widespread use (see Figure 3.1), most songs were built from the ground up by first recording the rhythm section of bass and drums (sometimes only the drums), and then adding everything else through a series of overdubs. This practice continues today.

The emphasis shifted from the bass being the foundation of the song to the drums. Up until the end of the '60s, the bass was considered the most important instrument in the mix and everything was built around it. Beginning with the later Beatle and Pink Floyd albums, the drums came to the forefront, thanks to individual miking (the drums where miked with only two mics previously). Today, more attention is given to the drum sound than ever before.

Exercise Pod - Identifying Different Recording Techniques And Eras

E3.1: Play any song from the 1950s or early '60s.

   A) Notice how everything seems small and the instruments aren't that distinct? Notice how thin the sound is?

   B) Now play any song from the '70s to today. Notice how much bigger it sounds? Notice how you can hear every instrument more distinctly?

E3.2: Play any song from the 1950s or early '60s.

   A) Notice how the bass is at the forefront of the mix? Listen to where the drums are in relation to the other instruments in the mix.

   B) Now play any song from the '70s to today. Notice where the drums are in the mix.

What Are You Trying To Accomplish?

When asked what you're trying to accomplish when mixing, it's easy to say, "I'm just trying to balance everything together." Sure, that's one aspect of it, but that's not all. If you were to analyze it, mixing comes down to three things:

- Developing the groove

- Emphasizing the most important elements

- Putting the performers in an environment

Let's look at each one.

Developing The Groove

The groove is the pulse of the song. It's that undeniable feeling that makes you want to get off your seat and shake your booty. You don't have to know what it is as much as recognize it when it's there, or when it's not. Despite what you might think, it's not only dance music that has a groove. Every kind of music, regardless if it's R&B, jazz, rock, country, or some alien space music, has a groove, but the better the music is performed, the "deeper" the groove is.

Contrary to popular belief, a groove doesn't have to have perfect time because *a groove is created by tension against even time*. As a result, the playing doesn't have to be perfect, it just has to be even in its execution. In fact, music loses its groove if it's too perfect, which is why a song can sound lifeless after it's been quantized in a workstation. It's lost its groove.

Another misconception is that the groove always comes from the drums and bass together. It could come from other instruments as well. Some songs, like the Police's "Every Breath You Take" have the rhythm guitar establish the groove, while most of the Motown hits of the '60s relied on James Jamerson's bass.

Regardless what instrument is providing the groove of the song, if you want a great mix, you've got to find it and develop it first before you do anything else.

Exercise Pod - Identifying The Groove

E3.3: In order to hear a groove at its best, let's go to the masters.

A) Play any song by James Brown, Prince, Sly and the Family Stone or George Clinton. Can you feel the pulse of the song, the groove?

B) Can you identify the instruments that are providing the groove?

E3.4: Pick one of your favorite songs and have a listen.

A) Can you feel the pulse of the song? What instrument(s) are providing the groove?

B) Play a song at random. Can you feel the pulse of the song? What instrument(s) are providing the groove?

C) Play a song from a genre that you seldom listen to. Can you feel the pulse of the song? What instrument(s) are providing the groove?

E3.5: Now listen to all of those songs again. What makes the groove stand out? Is it the balance of the instruments? Is it because the instruments providing the groove are louder? Is it the tone of the instruments? Are they punchier sounding than the others?

Emphasizing The Most Important Elements

Every song has some element that acts like a hook to capture a listener's attention. Many times it's the vocal but it can be other elements as well. Usually it's an element that's so important that without it, the song just wouldn't be the same. It could be like the piano line in Coldplay's "Clocks," the clavinet in Stevie Wonder's "Superstition," or the intro guitar line in the Rolling Stones' seminal "Satisfaction," where if they weren't there, it would almost be a different song.

Finding the most important mix element is vital to getting a great mix. That element provides the excitement and the reason to listen. In a dance song it might be the kick drum, in an R&B song it could be the groove, in a pop song it might be an interesting hook that an instrument plays in the intro and interludes, and yes, it could be the vocal in just about any genre. The thing is, you have to listen to each of the elements to discover exactly what the element is that drives the song. Once that element is found, make sure it's emphasized. You'll see how in the chapters after this.

Exercise Pod - Identifying The Most Important Song Element

E3.6: Pick one of your favorite songs and have a listen.

A) What instrument(s) is the most important? Would the song be different if it wasn't there?

B) Play a song at random. What instrument(s) is the most important? Would the song be different if it wasn't there?

C) Play a song from a genre that you seldom listen to. What instrument(s) is the most important? Would the song be different if it wasn't there?

Putting The Performers In An Environment

Nothing sounds more boring and more like a demo than a flat recording where the musicians sound like they're playing in a closet right next to you. Not only is it unnatural sounding, but it's usually not that exciting to the ear. If you go listen to any concert or live music in a club, it's the ambience of the space that makes it come alive.

That's why it's important to learn to how to put each element into its own environment, either by placement when recording or artificially when mixing. While it's easy to think that we're just talking about reverb and delay here, that's not the case. It's the concept of "tall, deep, and wide."

In order to do a great mix you must think in three dimensions: "tall, deep and wide." This means that all the frequencies of the audio spectrum are represented, the mix has some ambient depth, and it has some stereo width from left to right.

The "tall" or frequency dimension comes from knowing what frequencies are missing or are too predominant, which means that all of the sparkly, tinkly highs and fat, powerful lows are there, and that all instruments can be distinctly heard.

The "deep" or effects dimension is achieved by introducing new ambience elements into the mix. This is usually done with reverbs and delays (and other effects like flanging and chorusing), but room mics, overheads and even leakage play an equally big part as well.

The "wide" or panning dimension comes from placing a musical element in a sound field in such a way that it becomes a more interesting soundscape, and as a result, each element is heard more clearly.

Exercise Pod - Identifying The Tall, Deep And Wide Dimensions

E3.7: Pick one of your favorite songs and have a listen.

A) What instrument(s) contain the highest frequencies? What instruments contain the lowest frequencies? What instruments are mostly midrange?

B) What instrument(s) have the most ambience?

C) Does it seem to have a wide stereo field or is it closer to mono?

E3.8: Play a song at random.

A) What instrument(s) contain the highest frequencies? What instruments contain the lowest frequencies? What instruments are mostly midrange?

B) What instrument(s) have the most ambience?

C) Does it seem to have a wide stereo field or is it closer to mono?

E3.9: Play a song from a genre that you seldom listen to.

A) What instrument(s) contain the highest frequencies? What instruments contain the lowest frequencies? What instruments are mostly midrange?

B) What instrument(s) have the most ambience?

C) Does it seem to have a wide stereo field or is it closer to mono?

What Does An Amateur Mix Sound Like?

Before we can talk about how to make a great mix, it's good to be aware of the signs of one that isn't that great. Does your mix have any of these characteristics?

No contrast. The same ambient texture (as in the same reverb) is used throughout the entire song.

No focal point. There are holes between lyrics where nothing is brought forward in the mix to hold the listener's attention.

It's noisy. Clicks, hums, extraneous noises, count-offs, and sometimes lip-smacks and breaths are all signs of an amateur mix.

It lacks clarity and punch. Instruments aren't distinct, and the low end is either too weak or too big.

It sounds distant. The mix sounds distant because too much reverb or other effects have been used.

The element levels are inconsistent. Instrument levels vary from balanced to soft or too loud. Certain lyrics that can't be distinguished.

The sounds are dull and uninteresting. Generic, dated or often-heard sounds are used. There's a difference between using something because it's hip and new, and using it because everyone else is using it.

The 6 Elements Of A Mix

Every genre of music that has a strong backbeat has six main elements to a great mix. They are:

Balance: the volume level relationship between musical elements.

Frequency Range: the ability to hear each element clearly and have all the frequencies of the audio spectrum properly represented.

Panorama: placement of a musical element within the soundfield.

Dimension: the addition of ambience to a musical element.

Dynamics: control of the volume envelope of a track or instrument.

Interest: making the mix special.

It's possible to mix a song and only have four or five of these elements, but a great music mix contains all six, since they're all equally important (see Figure 3.2).

There are certain types of music that require the mixer to simply recreate an unaltered acoustic event like classical, jazz, or a live concert recording, so sometimes only the first four elements are needed to have a mix to be considered great. That being said, dynamics and interest have evolved to become extremely important elements as modern music has evolved.

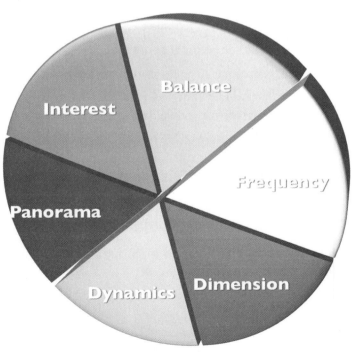

Figure 3.2: The 6 Elements Of A Mix

Exercise Pod - The Elements Of A Mix

E3.10: A) Listen to one of your favorite songs. Listen to the balance of the mix. What's in the forefront? What's in the background? How loud is the vocal compared to the instruments? Is the kick drum louder than the bass? Does the snare drum drive the song?

B) Now listen to a song at random. Listen to the balance of the mix. What's in the forefront? What's in the background? How loud is the vocal compared to the instruments? Is the kick drum louder than the bass? Does the snare drum drive the song?

C) Listen to a song from a genre that you're unfamiliar with. Listen to the balance of the mix. What's in the forefront? What's in the background? How loud is the vocal compared to the instruments? Is the kick drum louder than the bass? Does the snare drum drive the song?

E3.11: A) Go back and listen to that same favorite song. Listen to the frequency response of the mix. What instruments have lots of high-end? What instruments are mid-range heavy? What instruments have a lot of low end? What is the tone of the vocal? Are all the instruments defined and clearly heard?

B) Now listen to that song you picked at random. Listen to the frequency response of the mix. What instruments have lots of high-end? What instruments are mid-range heavy? What instruments have a lot of low end? What is the tone of the vocal? Are all the instruments defined and clearly heard?

C) Listen to that song from a genre that you're unfamiliar with. Listen to the frequency response of the mix. What instruments have lots of high-end? What instruments are mid-range heavy? What instruments have a lot of low end? What is the tone of the vocal? Are all the instruments defined and clearly heard?

E3.12: A) Go back and listen to that same favorite song. Where are all the instruments placed in the stereo field? What instruments are placed in the center? Is there an instrument that's panned to one side with an effect panned to the other? Are there instruments that are doubled and panned to either side? Are there instruments panned all the way to the left or right?

B) Now listen to that song you picked at random. Where are all the instruments placed in the stereo field? What instruments are placed in the center? Is there an instrument that's panned to one side with an effect panned to the other? Are there instruments that are doubled and panned to either side? Are there instruments panned all the way to the left or right?

C) Listen to that song from a genre that you're unfamiliar with. Where are all the instruments placed in the stereo field? What instruments are placed in the center? Is there an instrument that's panned to one side with an effect panned to the other? Are there instruments that are doubled and panned to either side? Are there instruments panned all the way to the left or right?

E3.13: A) Go back and listen to that same favorite song. What instruments or vocals seem dry and in your face? What instruments or vocals can you hear reverb on? What instruments or vocals can you hear delayed? Is the delay repeating? Does the snare drum have an effect on it? Does the vocal have an effect on it? Can you hear any chorus or flanging on any of the instruments?

B) Now listen to that song you picked at random. What instruments or vocals seem dry and in your face? What instruments or vocals can you hear reverb on?

What instruments or vocals can you hear delayed? Is the delay repeating? Does the snare drum have an effect on it? Does the vocal have an effect on it? Can you hear any chorus or flanging on any of the instruments?

C) Listen to that song from a genre that you're unfamiliar with. What instruments or vocals seem dry and in your face? What instruments or vocals can you hear reverb on? What instruments or vocals can you hear delayed? Is the delay repeating? Does the snare drum have an effect on it? Does the vocal have an effect on it? Can you hear any chorus or flanging on any of the instruments?

E3.14: A) Go back and listen to that same favorite song. Does the mix breathe in volume or does it seem compressed? Does the vocal sound compressed or natural? Does the kick and snare sound compressed or natural? Are there any instruments that sound overly compressed? Is there an instrument that sounds like it needs more compression?

B) Now listen to that song you picked at random. Does the mix breathe in volume or does it seem compressed? Does the vocal sound compressed or natural? Does the kick and snare sound compressed or natural? Are there any instruments that sound overly compressed? Is there an instrument that sounds like it needs more compression?

C) Listen to that song from a genre that you're unfamiliar with. Does the mix breathe in volume or does it seem compressed? Does the vocal sound compressed or natural? Does the kick and snare sound compressed or natural? Are there any instruments that sound overly compressed? Is there an instrument that sounds like it needs more compression?

E3.15: A) Go back and listen to that same favorite song. What's the most interesting element in the song? Is there a hook that grabs you? Is it a vocal or instrumental hook? Is it an effect?

B) Now listen to that song you picked at random. What's the most interesting element in the song? Is there a hook that grabs you? Is it a vocal or instrumental hook? Is it an effect?

C) Listen to that song from a genre that you're unfamiliar with. What's the most interesting element in the song? Is there a hook that grabs you? Is it a vocal or instrumental hook? Is it an effect?

CHAPTER 4
BALANCE

The essence of mixing is the balance between instruments or mix elements. No matter how good you are at other aspects of the mixing process, if you don't get the balance right, you don't have a mix. Before we begin mixing, let's look at some balancing concepts that are important to grasp.

Visualize Your Mix

Most mixers can hear some version of the final product in their heads before they get too far into the mix. This is because they've heard rough mixes of the song many times before during production, but even if a mixer is brought in just for the mix, they listen to all the elements several times before they really get down to mixing.

If you're just starting out mixing, you might think, "How can I hear the final product before I've even begin?" That's a fair enough question. Until you have a certain amount of experience, you need a few questions to help mold your vision a bit, and the way to do that is to go back to the six mix elements and ask yourself:

- How do I hear the final balance?

- How do I hear the instruments EQed?

- How do I hear everything panned?

- How do I hear everything compressed?

- How do I hear the ambience in the track?

- What do I hear as the most interesting thing in the track?

If you can answer these questions, you may still not have a full picture of your final mix, but you'll have at least a general idea, which is the first step to a great mix.

Keep in mind that the producer and musicians have a say in the mix as well, and your version of the mix can suddenly take a wide left turn with their input. That's okay, because after you've gotten everything to the point where you hear it in your head (or even beyond), a left turn should be easy.

Exercise Pod - Visualize Your Mix

E4.1: Either listen to a rough mix of the song you're working on, or quickly just push up all the faders for a rough balance to the song you're about to mix. Let's think about the balance.

A) How loud do you hear the drums in the final mix? The bass?

B) Do you hear the vocals out in front, or back in the track?

C) How loud do you hear the primary musical elements that carry the song?

D) How loud do you hear the secondary elements like percussion and background vocals?

E4.2: Now let's think about the frequency response of the various instruments.

A) Is there an instrument or two that sounds particularly dull?

B) Is there an instrument or two that sounds overly bright?

C) Is there an instrument that has too much bottom end?

D) Is there an instrument that has no bottom end at all?

E4.3: Now let's think about the panning.

A) How do you hear the drums panned? Wide or narrow?

B) How do you hear the panning of any instruments that were recorded in stereo?

C) Do you hear any instruments panned extreme wide left and right?

D) What instruments do you hear panned up the middle?

E4.4: Now let's go to compression.

A) Is there an instrument or vocal that has wild dynamic shifts that needs compression?

B) Is there an instrument or vocal that you'd like to change the sound of by using compression?

C) Is there an instrument or vocal that needs to sound a little more punchy?

E4.5: Let's think about the ambience.

A) What instruments were recorded with room ambience or reverb?

B) Do you hear ambience on the drums or snare?

C) What instruments do you hear rather dry and in your face?

D) What instruments do you hear further away from you?

E4.6: Lastly, it's time to think about the interest.

A) What's the most important element in the mix?

B) If there isn't one yet, how can I create one?

C) What's the next most important element in the mix?

D) What's the next most important element in the mix?

These aren't all the questions that you can ask yourself about a mix, but you get the idea. Remember, there are no right-or-wrong answers. It's as you visualize it in your head.

The Musical Elements Of An Arrangement

You read about the six elements of a mix in the last chapter, now let's look at the five elements of an arrangement. The arrangement of the song is so important because that's where the balance really begins. In a well-arranged song, you'll frequently find that it will almost mix itself. If the arrangement is, shall we say "less than adequate," you can fight and fight to fit everything in to make all the instruments seem like they belong together. That's why it's important to not only balance what you hear, but control what you don't hear as well. That means that sometimes muting a track is just as important to the mix as moving the faders.

So how does that relate to the arrangement? The number of musical elements that occur at the same time is critical to the attention of the listener. Too many, and the listener gets confused, fatigued, and moves on. That's why it's important for the mixer to have no more than five arrangement elements happening at the same time. These elements are:

The Foundation: The foundation is the instrument or instruments that provide the groove of the song. It's usually the bass and drums, but can also include a rhythm guitar and/or keys if they're playing the same rhythmic figure as the rhythm section.

The Pad: A pad is a long sustaining note or chord. Organs, electric pianos, synthesizers, strings and even guitar power chords are the typical instrument pads that you'll find in a mix.

The Rhythm: The rhythm is any instrument that adds motion and excitement to the track. A double time shaker or tambourine, a rhythm guitar strumming on the backbeat, or congas playing a Latin feel are all common examples of rhythm elements.

The Lead: A lead vocal, lead instrument, or instrumental solo.

The Fills: Fills generally occur in the spaces between Lead lines, or answer to the Lead. A common fill element can also be a signature line in an intro or interlude.

Most of the time, a song has only four or even three arrangement elements occurring at the same time, with the fills or the pad most likely to be left out.

You might think that about all the songs these days have a lot more than five tracks (some as many as a hundred), so how does this work in the real world? An element can be a single instrument like a lead guitar or a vocal, or it can be a group of instruments like the bass and drums, a doubled guitar line, a group of backing vocals, etc. **Generally, a group of instruments playing exactly the same rhythm is considered an element.** For example, a doubled lead guitar is a single element, as is a doubled lead vocal, or a lead vocal with two additional harmony vocals. Two lead guitars playing different parts are two elements, however. A lead and a rhythm guitar are also two separate elements as well (see Figure 4.1).

Just so you can understand the arrangement elements of a song, let's look at a few examples.

ELEMENT	PURPOSE	TYPICAL INSTRUMENTS
Foundation	The instruments that provide the groove or pulse of the song	Drums and bass
Pad	Long sustaining notes that glue the mix elements together	Organ, electric piano, strings, guitar power chords
Rhythm	The instruments that provide motion to the song	Percussion, rhythm guitar
Lead	The focal point of the song	Lead vocal, lead or solo instrument
Fill	The instruments that fill in the spaces between the lead phrases	Solo instrument, background vocal

Figure 4.1: The Arrangement Elements

"Born This Way" by Lady Gaga

- **The Foundation:** Like most songs, it's the bass and drums.

- **The Pad:** Like most dance songs, it's a synth pad that you can hear predominantly in the first verse, but it's there for the whole song, adding the glue to the tracks.

- **The Rhythm:** This element utilizes an aggressive synth with a saw-tooth wave shape that you can hear predominantly in the second half of the first verse.

- **The Lead:** As almost always, it's the lead vocal.

- **The Fills:** Like most hit pop songs, there's something in almost every space where there's not a vocal. Usually it's some sort of synth but there are lots of sound effects as well.

"Power" by Kanye West

- **The Foundation:** This one's easy, since it's the pretty standard bass and drums.

- **The Rhythm:** The rhythm element is an instrument that pushes the track along, usually double time or a complementary rhythm to the foundation. In this song it's the rap itself.

- **The Pad:** This is highly unusual in that it's a sampled background-vocal track that's repeated from the intro through most of the song.

- **The Lead:** As almost always, it's the lead vocal.

• **The Fills:** There are a lot of musical fills or contrary lines in this song, and there's not much room for them to stand by themselves. That's OK, because the mix is skillful enough to make them work.

"Grenade" by Bruno Mars

• **The Foundation:** As is the norm, the Foundation element is this song is held down by the bass and drums.

• **The Pad:** There's an organ that plays just underneath everything that acts as the pad and glues the track together. Once again, pretty standard. You can never go wrong with an organ for this element.

• **The Rhythm:** This is interesting in that the arpeggiated electric piano line in the verse acts as the rhythm element, but during the chorus it switches to the double-time feel of the drums.

• **The Lead:** As almost always, it's the lead vocal.

• **The Fill:** The Fills are handled by the background vocals and the occasional percussion sound effect.

Exercise Pod - Identifying Arrangement Elements

E4.7: Listen to your favorite song. Can you identify:

    A) the foundation?

    B) the pad?

    C) the rhythm?

    D) the lead?

    E) the fills?

E4.8: Listen to a song at random. Can you identify:

    A) the foundation?

    B) the pad?

    C) the rhythm?

    D) the lead?

    E) the fills?

E4.9: Listen to the song you're about to mix. Can you identify:

    A) the foundation?

    B) the pad?

    C) the rhythm?

    D) the lead?

    E) the fills?

Building The Mix

Despite what you might think, there is no standard instrument to start and build a mix from. Modern mixers employ various techniques and they're all valid, especially in different genres of music. For instance, here are the places from which a mix can be started:

- From the Bass.

- From the Kick Drum.

- From the Snare Drum.

- From the Drum Overheads.

- From the Lead Vocal or main instrument.

- With all of the instruments and vocals in right from the beginning.

- When mixing a string section, from the highest string (violin) to the lowest (bass).

There are some mixers who just push up all the faders and mix with everything in from the beginning. The theory here is that everything will eventually be in the mix anyway, so you might as well start with it all in as soon as you can. The advantage to this method is that by hearing all the instruments and vocals, you're able to make an aural space for everything. If you insert one instrument at a time, you begin to run out of space and frequently have to go back to the beginning to make sure everything fits together properly.

Whichever way you do it is fine; there is no right way or wrong way to build a mix. The method explained in the following exercises is frequently used, but feel free to change the order if it feels better to you.

Wherever you start from, it's a good idea that the lead arrangement element (usually the vocal) be inserted into the mix as soon as possible. Since the vocal is the most important element, it will use up more frequency space than other supporting instruments. Many mixers find that by waiting until late in the mix to put the vocal in, there's not enough space left and the vocal just never sits right with the rest of the track.

In our next exercise pod we'll experiment with different methods of getting a mix balance where we'll look at all of these methods.

The Drums

In the early days of recording there was no such thing as balancing the drums because the entire kit was treated as a single instrument and miked with just a single mic. As producers began to understand how important the beat was, a mic was added to the kick. Eventually the modern drum sound evolved to where each drum and sometimes each cymbal is individually miked. As a result, the internal mix of the drums is a very important part of virtually every modern recording.

Different engineers approach this mix in different ways. Some begin with the kick drum and build around that, while others start with the snare, since it provides the backbeat of most songs. Yet others want to build their drum mix around the toms so they don't get lost in the mix, especially if they're prominently featured.

A unique case has the mix being built around the overhead mics. The overhead mics are placed further away from the cymbals than normal cymbal miking, and are meant to pick up the overall sound of the drum kit. If overheads are used, many mixers like to start their mix from there and then fill in the sound with the other drum mics. This won't work so well when the mics are placed lower with the idea of just picking up the cymbals.

Setting The Levels

Wherever you start your mix from, keep in mind that the mix buss level will get louder and louder with every instrument entrance. That's why it's best to begin your mix with the mix bus meter (the master meters) reading at about -10 dB regardless of what instrument you start off with. With each instrument that enters at the same level as the current mix, the master mix meter should raise about 3 dB. Also remember that the sound of every drum will change anywhere from a little to a lot when a new drum or cymbal is added to the mix due to the leakage of the other drums into the mic.

Let's try all the starting places so you can get a feel for how each method works.

Exercise Pod - Balancing The Drums
Open up Example 1 on the DVD that accompanies this book.

E4.10: Building From The Kick

A) Raise the level of the kick drum until it reads about -10 dB on the master mix bus meter.

B) Raise the level of the snare until it's about the same level. Did the sound of the kick change when it was paired with the snare? Is the kick masked by the snare and no longer distinct? How high does the master mix bus meter read?

C) Go to a place in the song where there are tom fills. Raise the level of all toms until they're about the same level as the kick and snare. Did the sound of the kick and/or snare change? Does the kick and snare sound different when the toms aren't playing? How high does the master mix bus meter read?

D) Raise the level of the cymbal or overhead mics until the overall sound begins to change and the cymbals become more distinct sounding. What happened to the sound of the other drums? How high does the master mix bus meter read?

E) Raise the level of the hi-hat mic until it becomes a bit more distinct sounding. Does the sound of the snare change? Does the sound of any of the toms or cymbals change? How high does the master mix bus meter read?

E4.11: Building From The Snare

A) Raise the level of the snare drum until it reads about -10 dB on the master mix bus meter.

B) Raise the level of the kick until it's about the same level. Did the sound of the snare change when it was paired with the kick? Is the snare sound masked by the kick and no longer distinct? How high does the master mix bus meter read?

C) Go to a place in the song where there are tom fills. Raise the level of all toms until they're about the same level as the kick and snare. Did the sound of the kick and/or snare change? What do the kick and snare sound like when the toms aren't playing? How high does the master mix bus meter read?

D) Raise the level of the cymbal or overhead mics until the overall sound begins to change and the cymbals become more distinct sounding. What happened to the sound of the other drums? How high does the master mix bus meter read?

E) Raise the level of the hi-hat mic until it becomes a bit more distinct sounding. Does the sound of the snare change? How about any of the toms or cymbals? How high does the master mix bus meter read?

E4.12: Building From The Toms

A) Go to a place in the song where there are tom fills. Raise the level of the toms until they read about -10 dB on the master mix bus meter.

B) Raise the level of the kick until it's about the same level. Did the sound of the toms change when it was paired with the kick? Do the kick and toms blend or is one covered up? How high does the master mix bus meter read?

C) Raise the level of the snare until it's about the same level as the toms. Did the sound of the kick or toms change when the snare entered? How high does the master mix bus meter read?

D) Raise the level of the cymbal or overhead mics until the overall sound begins to change and the cymbals become more distinct sounding. What happened to the sound of the toms? How high does the master mix bus meter read?

E) Raise the level of the hi-hat mic until it becomes a bit more distinct sounding. Does the sound of any of the toms change? How about the snare? How high does the master mix bus meter read?

E4.13: Building From The Overhead Mics

A) Raise the level of the overhead mics until they read about -10 dB on the master mix bus meter. Can you hear all the drums? Are they all balanced?

B) Raise the level of the kick drum until it's just louder than what you heard from the overhead mics. Did the sound of the overhead mics change? How high does the master mix buss meter read?

C) Raise the level of the snare until it's just louder than what you heard from the overhead mics. Did the sound of the overhead mics change when the snare entered? How high does the master mix bus meter read?

D) Go to a place in the song where there are tom fills. Raise the level of all toms until they're just higher than what you heard in the overhead mics. Did the sound of the overall drum kit change? What does everything sound like when the toms aren't playing? How high does the master mix bus meter read?

E) Raise the level of the hi-hat mic until it becomes a bit more distinct sounding. Does the sound of the snare change? How about any of the toms or cymbals? How high does the master mix bus meter read?

Checking The Drum Phase

One of the most important yet overlooked parts of a drum mix is checking the phase of the drums. This is important because not only will an out-of-phase channel suck the low end out of the mix, but it will get more difficult to fix as the mix progresses.

A drum mic can be out of phase due to a mis-wired cable or poor mic placement. Either way, it's best to fix it now before the mix goes any further.

Figure 4.2: A Channel Phase Control

Exercise Pod - Checking The Drum Phase

E4.14: A) With all the drums in the mix, go to the kick drum channel and change the selection of the polarity or phase control (see Figure 4.2). Is there more low end or less? Chose the selection with the most bottom end.

B) Go to the snare drum channel and change the selection of the polarity or phase control. Is there more low end or less? Chose the selection with the most bottom end.

C) Go to each tom mic channel and change the selection of the polarity or phase control. Is there more low end or less? Chose the selection with the most bottom end.

D) Go to each cymbal mic or overhead mic and change the selection of the polarity or phase control. Is there more low end or less? Chose the selection with the most bottom end.

Assigning The Drums To A Group Or Subgroup

Whenever there are two or more instruments of a mix element, like a drum kit, five guitars, six background vocals, or eight percussion tracks, it's best to assign them to either a group or a subgroup in order to make mix any adjustments that you might have to make later somewhat easier. The difference between a group and a subgroup is that in a group, a number of channel faders (like the drums) are electronically or digitally chained together. When you move one fader in the group, they all move, yet keep the same relative balance that you originally set.

A subgroup has the same effect yet works a little differently. All of the channels of the group are assigned to a subgroup fader, which is then assigned to the master mix bus. The level of the all of the channels is controlled with that one fader, and if you move any fader within the group, the others don't move with it but you change the balance of the mix. If you send to an effect or insert a compressor from the subgroup it also affects all the instruments in that group, which can be a benefit in certain situations during mixing.

Exercise Pod - Assigning The Drum Channels To A Subgroup

E4.15: A) On your DAW, assign all of the drum channels to a group. Move one of the faders. Do all the faders move yet keep the same balance relationship?

B) On your console or DAW, assign all of your drum channels to a subgroup. Raise or lower the subgroup fader. Does the level of the drums get louder and softer?

The Bass

The balance between the bass and drums is critical because it provides the power of the mix. Where once upon a time the bass amp was always miked, today most basses are taken direct, but sometimes both the amp mic and the direct signals are recorded on separate tracks as well. This might occur so that the bass sound has the best combination of bottom end and clarity.

Just like the drums, the phase between the direct bass sound and the miked one must be checked if they've both been recorded, or the bass sound may sound thin with no power.

Sometimes a bass that sounds on the small side will sound a lot fuller when combined with the kick. That's why it's important to listen to the kick and bass together.

Exercise Pod - Balancing The Bass And Drums

E4.16: Check the phase between the bass amp and direct signal.

A) Raise the level of the direct signal until it reads -10 dB on the mix bus meter.

B) Mute the direct signal and raise the level of the amp signal until it also reads -10 dB on the mix bus meter.

C) Un-mute the direct signal. The direct and amp signals should now be exactly the same level.

D) Change the selection of the polarity or phase control on the amp mic channel. Is there more low end or less? Chose the selection with the most bottom end.

E4.17: Balance the bass channels.

A) Pick whatever channel you think sounds best and raise the level so it reads -10 dB on the master mix bus meter.

B) Slowly raise the level of the second bass channel. Does the bass sound fuller and fatter? Does it sound clear and distinct?

C) Set it where you think it sounds best for now. This balance will be adjusted later when more instruments are introduced into the mix.

D) Assign the bass channels to a group or subgroup.

E4.18: Balance the bass and drums.

A) Using your final drum mix from before, mute all the drums except the kick. It should read about -10 dB on the mix bus meter. Now mute the channel.

B) Raise the bass group or subgroup channel until the master mix bus meter reads -10 dB. Now un-mute the kick drum channel. Does the kick and bass sound like they're at about the same level? What does the master mix bus meter read?

C) Un-mute the other drum channels so you hear the entire drum kit and the bass. Does the bass sit well with the drums? Can you hear the kick, snare and bass distinctly? Don't worry if you can't. We'll fix it later with the EQ.

The Vocals

Many mixers like to get the vocal in the mix as soon as possible, because if you wait until the end after you've mixed all the music, the balance changes after the vocal is put into the mix. Plus, the vocal is usually the focal point of the song, so it's best to get that sounding great and build around it.

Since the '60s, doubling a vocal has been an effective way to make it sound better and even out any tuning inconsistencies. There are two ways to treat vocal doubling; set both vocals at the same level, or set one about -10 dB less than the lead vocal and use it for support.

Background Vocals

Most of the trick to background vocals has more to do with panning, equalization, and effects than it does with balance, but let's look at a couple of scenarios where balance does come into play.

Harmony Vocals: With harmony vocals, the balance is crucial in order to get the correct blend and impact. Usually the highest vocal cuts pretty well, but the lowest or one in the middle of a three-part harmony gets lost. If the lowest part of the three-part harmony is the melody, then it's usually the middle part that gets lost.

The easiest (but not the only) way to balance three-part harmony is to begin just like you did with the rhythm section, from the bottom up. Start with the lowest vocal, add the middle vocal until the blend is such that they sound as one, then add the highest vocal part.

Make sure to assign the background vocal channels to either a group or a subgroup.

Gang Vocals: Gang vocals are shouts or a unison vocal part where the balance isn't as important to attain a blend as with harmony vocals. If well recorded, the gang vocal will have a lot of different types of voices, and/or a lot of different natural room ambience, because some may have been recorded further from the mic.

There are two ways to approach balance in this situation. If you have a lot of voices with different timbres, once again start from the lowest to the highest, since the highest sounding voices will cut through the mix easier. If you have voices with different room ambiences, start with the one that sounds furthest away to get the biggest sound.

Exercise Pod - Balancing The Lead And Background Vocals
E4.19: Balance the lead vocal with the rhythm section.

A) Raise the level of the lead vocal until it's the loudest musical element. This is common in pop songs. Does the vocal overpower the rhythm section?

B) Now adjust the level of the lead vocal so it's only as loud, or even a little softer, than the bass and drums. This will emphasize the band and make it more powerful. Can you still hear every word of the vocal?

E4.20: Balance a vocal double.
There's not an example of this on the DVD, but here's what to try if one of your own songs has a doubled vocal.

A) After the vocal level is set as above, raise the level of the double until it's the same level as the lead vocal. Does the vocal sound louder? Is the vocal fuller sounding?

B) After the vocal level is set as above, raise the level of the double until it sits about -10 dB below the lead vocal, or loud enough that you can just hear it. Does the vocal sound louder? Is the vocal fuller sounding?

C) Assign both vocals to a group or subgroup and readjust the level and in exercise E4.19.

E4.21: Balance three-part harmony vocals.

A) With the background vocals soloed, raise the level of the lowest vocal, then the middle vocal, then the highest vocal. Do they blend so they sound like one voice?

B) Assign the background vocal channels to a group or subgroup, un-solo, and balance against the track.

E4.22: Balance gang vocals.

A) With the gang vocals soloed, raise the level of the lowest or deepest sounding vocal first, then add in all vocals in with the ones with the highest timbre last. Do they blend so they sound like one voice?

B) With the gang vocals soloed, raise the level of the vocal that sounds furthest away first, then add in all vocals with the closest sounding vocal last. Do they blend so they sound like one voice?

C) Assign the gang vocal channels to a group or subgroup, un-solo, and balance against the track.

Guitars

Guitars can make up every type of arrangement element, depending strictly upon the song. They can be part of the rhythm section, playing quarter notes with the snare drum, they can play big power chords that act as the pad of the song, or they can strum in double time to push the song along as the rhythm element. If that isn't enough, they can be the lead instrument in solos, intros, or in an instrumental, or be fills, playing in the holes around the vocal.

Often there are multiple guitar tracks layered to achieve a bigger sound, which can cause problems that can't always be taken care of by balance alone. Some frequency adjustment of the tracks, which we'll cover in Chapter 7, is required to keep them from fighting each other.

But by far, the primary task for the mixer is to identify exactly what arrangement element the guitar fits into, then balance it accordingly.

Exercise Pod - Balancing Guitars

E4.23: Using the first example on the DVD, listen to Guitar #1.

A) Does it belong to the rhythm section, is it a pad or rhythm element, or is it a lead or fill element?

B) Mix the guitar so it blends into the rhythm section. Does it still stick out?

C) Mix the guitar as if it were a rhythm element. Does it stick out of the track or blend in?

E4.24: Listen to the Guitar #2 in the bridge of the example. This is a guitar with power chords used as a pad.

A) Mix the guitar pad so it's down low in the track, just barely audible. Mute and un-mute it. Does the track sound fuller when it's un-muted? Does it stick out?

B) Mix the guitar pad so it's up front, almost as loud as the vocal. Does it take attention away from the vocal? Is the song still powerful or does it lose the groove? Does the track still sound full if you mute it?

E4.25: Listen to the third guitar in the example. It's a lead instrument in the intro, interlude and solo, and a fill element when used elsewhere.

A) Raise the level of the lead guitar until it's the loudest musical element. Does the vocal overpower the rhythm section?

B) Raise the level of the lead guitar so it's only as loud, or even a little softer, than the bass and drums. Does the track still have excitement when it plays?

E4.26: Guitars four and five are meant to be layered, meaning they sound better when played together than individually.

A) Raise the level so that you just hear guitar #4. Now solo it, then solo guitar #5 and raise its level until they blend together to sound like one instrument.

B) Un-solo both guitars and listen with the track. Is this element louder in the track than before? Does it blend into the track?

C) Assign both guitars to a group or subgroup so they're easier to control. Now set the balance so they're just audible in the track. Does the track seem fuller?

D) Now set the balance so it's about even with the vocal. Which element draws your attention to it? Is the rhythm section overpowered or do you still hear the groove of the song?

Keyboards

As with guitars, keyboards as a group can be a part of just about any arrangement element, but it's best that we separate keyboards into piano, organ, electric piano and synthesizers, since each does have a somewhat specific function. Depending upon what arrangement element the keyboard serves, it might be better to add it to the mix before the guitars. This is your preference, but also depends upon the song and arrangement as well.

Once again it's best to determine which arrangement element the instrument falls into, then balance it accordingly.

Piano

Since a grand or upright piano is very percussive in nature, it usually serves as either a foundation, rhythm, lead or fill arrangement element. It's possible that it can also be a pad, if it plays long sustaining chords.

Electric Piano

The electric piano seems made for the pad element since it's very mellow sounding, easily blends in with the track, and is capable of playing long sustaining chords. You may find it used as other elements as well, but not nearly as often as the pad.

Organ

The organ is the perfect pad element since it's capable of infinite sustaining chords. A Hammond organ is often used as the glue to a track, placed back in the mix where it's barely heard.

Synthesizers

Synths are another instrument that can also serve as any arrangement element. They can be very percussive and serve as a foundation element, or can simulate strings for a great pad.

Exercise Pod - Balancing The Keyboards

E4.27: Listen to the piano in the example.

A) Does it belong to the rhythm section, is it a pad or rhythm element, or is it a lead or fill element?

B) Mix the piano so it blends into the rhythm section. Does it still stick out?

C) Mix the piano low in the track as if it were a pad element. Does it stick out of the track or blend in?

D) Mix the piano as if it were a lead element. Does it stick out of the track or blend in?

E4.28: Listen to the electric piano in the example.

A) Does it belong to the rhythm section, is it a pad or rhythm element, or is it a lead or fill element?

B) Mix the electric piano so it blends into the rhythm section. Does it still stick out?

C) Mix the electric piano low in the track as if it were a pad element. Does it still stick out of the track or blend in?

D) Mix the electric piano as if it were a lead element. Does it stick out of the track or blend in?

E4.29: Listen to the organ in the example.

A) Does it belong to the rhythm section, is it a pad or rhythm element, or is it a lead or fill element?

B) Mix the organ so it blends into the rhythm section. Does it still stick out?

C) Mix the organ low in the track as if it were a pad element. Does it stick out of the track or blend in?

D) Mix the organ as if it were a lead element. Does it stick out of the track or blend in?

E4.30: Listen to the synthesizer in the example.

A) Does it belong to the rhythm section, is it a pad or rhythm element, or is it a lead or fill element?

B) Mix the synthesizer so it blends into the rhythm section. Does it still stick out?

C) Mix the synthesizer low in the track as if it were a pad element. Does it stick out of the track or blend in?

D) Mix the synthesizer as if it were a lead element. Does it stick out of the track or blend in?

Loops

Loops are a crucial musical element these days and generally change the way you build a track, depending upon the importance of the element. If a loop is present, it's usually best to start the mix with that element, then build the mix around it, since the loop can be considered a foundation arrangement element or part of the rhythm section. If the song is made up primarily of loops, then it's important to find the combination of loops that creates the groove, then build the mix from there.

Exercise Pod - Balancing Loops

E4.31: A) Raise the level of the loop until you just begin to hear it in the track. Does it belong to the rhythm section, is it a pad or rhythm element, or is it a lead or fill element?

B) Does it fight other instruments for space?

E4.32: A) Begin the entire mix again only starting with the loop first. Raise it so the level on the mix bus meter reads -10 dB, and add the other instruments as in the previous exercises.

B) Does the loop fit better into the mix now? Does the loop or the rhythm section provide the groove?

E4.33: Go the fourth song. This contains only loops.

A) Find the most important loop. The one that will serve as the foundation element. Raise it so the level reads -10 dB on the mix bus meter.

B) Listen to the other loops. Which one acts as the pad?

C) Listen to the other loops. Which one acts as the rhythm?

D) Listen to the other loops. Which one acts as the lead?

E) Listen to the other loops. Which are fills?

Mixing By Muting

It's not uncommon to work with an artist or band that isn't sure of the arrangement, or is into experimenting and just allows an instrument to play throughout the entire song. As a result, more than five arrangement elements

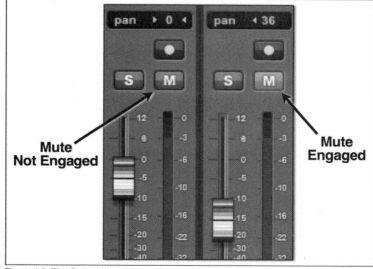

Figure 4.3: The Channel Mute Button

are present, or parts become inappropriate for the song in certain sections. This is where the mixer gets a chance to rearrange the track by keeping what works and muting the conflicting instrument or instruments (see Figure 4.3). Not only can the mixer influence the arrangement this way, but also the dynamics and general development of the song as well. In fact, sometimes the track that's muted becomes more important than if it were left playing. Always consider the mute buttons of the channels as a welcome feature that can help you bring your tracks together just as much as the faders.

Automation

Whether working on a real console or a console panel in your DAW, console automation is an extremely important function of your mix. Automation means that the console will remember your fader or parameter control moves and automatically perform them the next time the mix is played back.

Although most console parameters can now be automated in most DAW applications, the most primary is fader automation, which controls the balance between mix elements. Fader

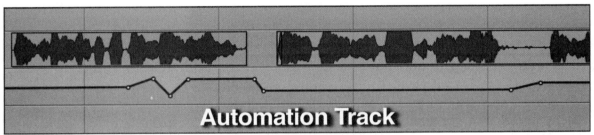

Figure 4.4: A Console Automation Track

automation allows you to perform minute fader moves to raise or lower the level of an instrument in a section, or even raise the level of a single syllable of a vocal so it can be better heard (Figure 4.4).

Automation is an essential part of tweaking a modern day mix, but it's by no means absolutely necessary. The airwaves are filled with hits mixed with no automation at all, although most of the songs had fewer tracks than we're used to dealing with today. That said, it's beyond the scope of this book to cover automation, since it's an advanced function and we're only covering the basics. Check out your console or DAW manual for detailed information as to how its automation works.

CHAPTER 5
PANNING

One of the most taken-for-granted elements in mixing is the placement of sound elements in the stereo soundfield, otherwise known as panning. Not only does stereo provide a sense of spaciousness, but it allows us to create excitement by adding movement within the stereo field, as well as adding clarity to an instrument by moving it out of the way of other sounds.

Moving a sound out of the way of another via the pan pot is really important in a mix. Sometimes just a little movement to the left and right will suddenly take a mix element from obscurity to definition. This works well with background and lead vocals, for example. When the lead and background vocals are panned in the center, each can obscure the other so that neither is heard very well. If the background vocals are moved a little out from the center, both can now be distinctly heard on their own.

The Three Main Panning Areas

There are three main areas of a stereo field that are used the most; hard left, hard right, and center. When the sound of an instrument comes out of both speakers at an equally loud level, it seems as if it's coming from in between them. This is what's known as the "phantom center." This phantom center can shift from left to right as you move your head around, which is why the exact center between the speakers where the phantom image is heard is called "the sweet spot" (see Figure 5.1).

The other two main panning areas are hard to the left, and hard to the right, which means you place the pan pot all the way to the left or right so the so sound only is heard in that one speaker.

Low Frequencies In The Center

In most mixes the prominent music element (usually the lead vocal or instrument) is panned in the center, but the kick drum, bass guitar and even the snare drum can be found there as well. Putting the bass and kick in the middle makes the mix feel strong and anchored, but this practice really comes from the era of vinyl records.

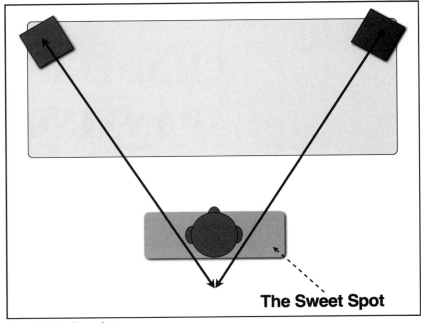

The Sweet Spot

Figure 5.1: The Sweet Spot

In the early days of stereo back in the mid-sixties, mixers only had three-way pan switches to pan with. These selected either the left, the right, or both speakers, which gave you the phantom center effect. The true pan pot that allowed you to place the instrument anywhere in between the speakers hadn't been invented yet. As a result, some of the early stereo records had the vocals on the left side and all the music on the right side, like on some of the early stereo releases by the Beatles.

The problem was that a mix with most of the low-frequency information on one side caused a lot of problems when making the vinyl record, causing it to skip. As a result, a special kind of equalizer (called an Elliptical EQ) was designed to filter all the low-frequency information and place it equally between the speakers in the center. Now it was possible to make a louder disc that had more bass than before, and the mixers discovered that the sound was more powerful as a result.

Today we don't have to worry about the limitations of the vinyl record anymore (unless that's your intended distribution medium), so it's possible to place the bass, kick drum, floor tom, or any instrument with a lot of low frequencies, anywhere in the stereo spectrum that we like, since it won't make a bit of difference to an MP3, AIFF file or a CD. Still, mixers everywhere place anything with low-frequency information in the center simply because it makes the mix sound much more powerful.

Panning The Drums

Back in the days when a drum kit was recorded with only a few microphones, the drums were recorded in mono, sometimes even on a single track. Today with most drum kits and drum loops tracked in stereo, the entire mix is built upon the idea that the drums will take up a lot of space in the stereo field.

There are two ways to pan the drums. Most mixers will pan it the way they see the kit set up, with the high hat slightly on the right and floor tom on the left for a right-handed player. A few mixers choose to pan from the drummers perspective, where everything is reversed.

Exercise Pod - Panning The Drums

E5.1: Begin with the mix that you achieved in the last chapter.

A) Pan the overhead mics hard to the left and right. What happens to the sound? What happens to the mix bus meters?

B) Now pan the overheads to the ten and two o'clock positions. What happens to the sound? What happens to the mix bus meters?

C) Pan the overheads both to the center. What happens to the sound? What happens to the mix bus meters?

D) Now reverse the position of the overheads so that the left is panned hard right and the right is panned hard left. What does it sound like? What happens to the mix bus meters?

E5.2: Pan the overheads back to the hard left and hard right positions as they should be.

A) Pan the kick to the hard left. What happens to the sound? What happens to the mix bus meters?

B) Pan the kick back to the center. What happens to the sound? What happens to the mix bus meters?

E5.3: A) Pan the snare to the hard right. What happens to the sound? What happens to the mix bus meters?

B) Pan the snare back to the center. What happens to the sound? What happens to the mix bus meters?

C) Pan the snare to about one o'clock position where it would sit if you were looking at it. What happens to the sound? What happens to the mix bus meters?

E5.4: A) Pan the high-hat hard to the left. What happens to the sound? What happens to the mix bus meters?

B) Pan the high-hat to the center. What happens to the sound? What happens to the mix bus meters?

C) Pan the high-hat to about two o'clock where it would sit if you were looking at it. What happens to the sound? What happens to the mix bus meters?

E5.5: Go to a place in the song with a drum fill.

A) Pan the right rack tom hard right, the left rack tom to the center, and the floor tom hard to the left. What does it sound like? What happens to the mix bus meters?

B) Pan the right rack tom to about the two o'clock position, the left rack tom to the ten o'clock position, and the floor tom hard to the left, where they would sit if you were looking at them. What does it sound like? What happens to the mix bus meters?

E5.6: A) If you have a song with stereo room mics, pan them hard left and hard right. What does it sound like? What happens to the mix bus meters?

B) Pan the room mics to the 10 and two o'clock positions. Does it have more or less power? What happens to the mix bus meters?

C) Pan both room mics to the center. Does it have more or less power? What happens to the mix bus meters?

Panning The Bass

The bass is another instrument with a lot of low frequencies that brings more power to the mix if it's panned in the center. Stereo bass is rarely, if ever, used.

Exercise Pod - Panning The Bass

E5.7: Begin with the mix that you achieved in the last chapter.

A Pan both the direct and miked bass hard to the left and right. What does it sound like? What happens to the mix bus meters?

B) Pan the bass tracks to the 10 and two o'clock positions. Does it have more or less power? What happens to the mix bus meters?

C) Now pan both channels to the center. Is the mix more powerful? What happens to the mix bus meters?

Panning Guitars

Guitar is an instrument that benefits greatly from panning. Sometimes just moving a guitar slightly in the stereo field will make the difference from it being masked or being heard.

Exercise Pod - Panning Guitars

E5.8: Begin with the mix that you achieved in the last chapter.

A) Un-mute Guitar #1. Pan it slightly left of center. Can you hear it better than before? What happens to the mix bus meters?

B) Pan Guitar #1 to the nine o'clock position. Can you hear it better than before? What happens to the mix bus meters?

C) Un-mute Guitar #2 and pan it to the three o'clock position. What does the mix sound like? What happens to the mix bus meters?

D) Pan Guitar #1 hard left and guitar #2 hard right. What does the mix sound like? Can you hear the guitars better? What happens to the mix bus meters?

E) Now add Guitar #3. Where can you pan it so you can hear it and the other instruments best?

Stereo Instruments

When an instrument is recorded in stereo, like a piano, a drum kit or doubled guitars, your first inclination is to pan everything hard left and hard right. Although that does give you the greatest stereo effect, that may not always be best for the mix.

Sometimes panning one side hard left, and the other at one o'clock, gives more room for other instruments to be panned to the right side (see Figure 5.2). Sometimes panning at ten and two o'clock is sufficient to hear the effect and keep some space open for other instruments. Sometimes even panning one side hard right and another to three o'clock will provide some stereo effect yet leave lots of space for other instruments. The key is to remember that just because it's in stereo doesn't mean that it has to be panned to the extreme left and right.

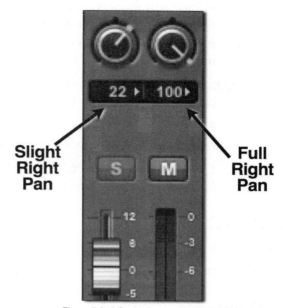

Figure 5.2: A Stereo Instrument With A Narrow Pan

Panning Keyboards

Most acoustic keyboards today are tracked in stereo. Pianos, organs, upright pianos, harpsichords and most other keyboard instruments all lend themselves to a wide stereo image because it usually takes multiple mics to properly capture all their range. Just because they're recorded in stereo doesn't mean that they have to be panned that way, however. Many times a stereo instrument panned in mono will sit much better in a mix.

Exercise Pod - Panning The Keyboards

E5.9: Begin with the mix that you achieved in the last chapter.

A) Pan the piano so that the low strings are panned hard left and the high strings are panned hard right. How does it sound in the mix? Can you hear the piano well or is it buried in the mix? What happens to the mix bus meters?

B) Reverse the panning so that the high end is panned hard left and the low end is panned hard right. How does the mix sound? Can you hear it well or is it buried in the mix? What happens to the mix bus meters? Does it sound as natural?

C) Pan both the high and low channels of the piano so that they're at the ten o'clock position in the stereo field. How does the mix sound? Can you hear it well or is it buried in the mix? What happens to the mix bus meters? Does it sound as natural as before?

D) If you move the pan of the piano around the stereo field, is there a place where you can hear it best? What happens to the mix bus meters?

Pseudo-Stereo

Most synthesizers and virtual instruments have a sort of pseudo-stereo effect that makes the instrument sound larger than it really is when panned hard left and right. The effect sounds great. It's big, it's wide, it's huge - all the things that an engineer loves during a mix. The problem is if you have a number of instruments that are all panned hard left and right on top of one another with the same type of effect, and the result is something called "big mono."

When big mono occurs, you're not creating much of a stereo spectrum because everything is placed hard left and right, and you're robbing the track of definition and depth because all of these tracks are panned on top of one another. The solution is to either throw away the track that has the warbled chorused sound, keep the dry one, and either pan in mono or make your own stereo element (which we'll cover in Chapter 9), or just find a place to pan everything inside the extreme left and right.

Exercise Pod - Pseudo-Stereo Panning

E5.10: Begin with the mix that you achieved in the last chapter.

A) Un-mute the synthesizer and pan it hard left and hard right. How does the mix sound? Can you hear the synth well or is it buried in the mix? What happens to the mix bus meters?

B) Pan both channels of the synth so that they're at the ten o'clock position in the stereo field. How does the mix sound? Can you hear it well or is it buried in the mix? What happens to the mix bus meters? Does it sound as natural?

C) Solo each channel of the synthesizer individually and find the one that warbles, indicating that it's chorused. Now mute that channel only. Un-solo the other synth channel and listen to it in the mix. How does the mix sound? Can you hear it well or is it buried in the mix? What happens to the mix bus meters? Does it sound as natural?

Panning Vocals

With few exceptions, most lead vocals are always panned to the center of the mix so the focus of attention is always on them. Background vocals, however, are a different story. It's not uncommon to spread background vocals almost anywhere in the stereo field in order to separate them from the vocal so they can be both heard clearly.

Exercise Pod - Panning The Lead Vocals

E5.11: Begin with the mix that you achieved in the last chapter.

A) Pan the lead vocal and the lead vocal double hard left and hard right. How does the mix sound? Can you hear the vocal well or is it buried in the mix? What happens to the mix bus meters?

B) Pan the lead vocal and the lead vocal double so they're at the ten o'clock and two o'clock position in the stereo field. How does the mix sound? Can you hear it well or is it buried in the mix? What happens to the mix bus meters?

C) Pan the lead vocal and the lead vocal double so that they're at the center position in the stereo field. How does the mix sound? Can you hear it well or is it buried in the mix? What happens to the mix bus meters?

Exercise Pod - Panning The Background Vocals

E5.12: Begin with the mix that you achieved in the last chapter.

A) Pan the background vocal tracks so that they're at the center position in the stereo field. How does the mix sound? Can you hear them well or are they buried in the mix? What happened to the mix bus meters?

B) Pan the background vocal tracks so that they're hard left and hard right in the stereo field. How does the mix sound? Can you hear the background vocals well or are they buried in the mix? What happened to the mix bus meters?

C) Pan the background vocal tracks so they're at the ten o'clock and two o'clock position in the stereo field. How does the mix sound? Can you hear them well or are they buried in the mix? What happened to the mix bus meters?

CHAPTER 6
COMPRESSION

In real life, music has a wide dynamic range that sometimes varies from an almost silent whisper to a spine-tingling roar. The problem is that vinyl records, CDs, radio, television, MP3s and just about any other kind of audio distribution media have dynamic ranges that just can't accommodate these wide swings in volume so common in normal life. In order to fit almost any kind of audio into the limited dynamic range of those media, there has to be some compression of that large dynamic range into something that fits the medium, and that's why we use a compressor.

This was more essential in the days of magnetic tape and vinyl records, but more modern formats like the CD and now online audio files have a much wider dynamic range, so the large amount of compression is no longer a necessity. The problem is that we have become accustomed to the sound of compressed audio, and now prefer to hear it that way.

As a result, today's compressors are used not only for the essential matter of dynamics control, but also for the sound that they impart, which is totally important to the mixing engineer.

Compression Basics
A compressor is nothing more than an automated level control that uses the input signal to determine the output level. Some models do this so transparently that you can't hear them working at all, while other models impart their own sound by just being inserted into the signal path. Regardless of how they sound, all have roughly the same parameter controls and are operated the same way.

Compressor Controls

Not every compressor has the same controls, although most of the modern hardware and plug-in models do. Let's look at these typical parameter controls.

Ratio

The *Ratio* parameter controls how much the output level of the compressor will increase compared to the level being fed to the input (see Figure 6.1). For instance, if the compression ratio is set at 4:1 (four to one), that means for every 4 dB of level that goes into the compressor, only 1 dB will come out once the signal reaches the threshold level (the point at which the compressor begins to work). If a compression ratio is set at 8:1, then for every 8 dB that goes into the unit, only 1 dB will come out of the output. On some compressors, the ratio control is fixed, but on most compressors the Ratio

parameter is variable from 1:1 (where there's no compression) to as much as 100:1 (where it then become a limiter, a subject that we'll address later in this chapter). Some compressors (like the famous UREI LA-2A - see Figure 6.2 - and LA-3) have a fixed ratio that gives it a particular sound.

Figure 6.1: Typical Compressor Controls

Threshold or Input

The *threshold* control determines the signal level where the compression begins (see Figure 6.1). Below the threshold point, no compression occurs. For instance, many compressors are calibrated in dB, so a setting of -5 dB means that when the level reaches -5 dB on the input meter, the compression begins to kick in.

Figure 6.2: A UREI/Teletronix LA-2A Compressor

Figure 6.3: A dbx 160A Compressor

Figure 6.4: The T-RackS Fairchild 670 Compressor Plug-in

Attack And Release

Most, but not all, compressors have *Attack* and *Release* parameter controls (see Figure 6.1). These controls determine how fast or slow the compressor reacts to the beginning (the attack) and end (the release) of the signal envelope. Many compressors have an *auto* mode that automatically sets the attack and release according to the dynamics of the signal. Although auto works relatively well, it still doesn't allow you to dial in the precise settings required by certain material sources. Some compressors (again like the famous UREI LA-2A or the dbx 160A - see Figure 6.3) have a fixed attack and release that can't be altered, which helps give the compressor a distinctive sound. Other compressors (like the famous Fairchild 670 - see Figure 6.4) have selectable attack and release parameters.

The *Attack* and *Release* controls are the key to proper compressor setup, but many engineers overlook these controls completely. It's possible to get good results by keeping these controls set to the mid-way position, but learning how to use them provides more much more consistent and professional results. We'll cover this soon.

Gain, Make-Up Gain or Output

When a compressor actually compresses the signal, the level is decreased, so there needs to be another parameter that boosts the signal back up to where it was before it was compressed. Depending upon the compressor, this parameter control is called either *Gain*, *Make-Up Gain* or *Output* (see Figure 6.1).

Figure 6.5: 4 dB Of Compression

Gain Reduction Meter

The gain reduction meter is an indicator of how much compression is occurring at any given moment (see Figure 6.1). On most devices this is shown via a VU or peak meter that reads backwards. In other words, it's set at zero and usually travels to the left into the minus range to show compression. As an example, a meter that reads -4 dB indicates that there is 4 dB of compression occurring at that time (see Figure 6.5)

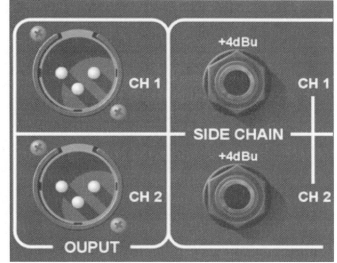

Figure 6.6: Compressor Side Chain Input And Output

The Side Chain

Many compressors also have an additional input and output called a side chain, which is used for connecting other signal processors to it (see Figure 6.6). The connected processor only receives the signal when the compressor exceeds the threshold and begins to compress. Side chains are often connected to EQs to make a *de-esser*, which will soften the loud "SSS" sounds from a vocalist when they exceed the compressor's threshold (we'll cover this a bit later). You can connect a delay, reverb or anything you want to a side chain for unusual, program-level-dependent effects. A side chain isn't needed for normal compressor operations, so many manufacturers choose not to include it on their units.

Bypass or In

Most compressors, especially most of the plug-in versions, have a *Bypass* control that allows you to hear the signal without any gain reduction taking place. This is useful to help you hear how much the compressor is controlling or changing the sound, or to make it easy to set the *Output* control so the compressed signal is the same level as the uncompressed signal.

Compressor Operation

Controlling dynamics means keeping the level of the sound even by lifting the level of the soft passages and lowering the level of the loud ones so that there's less of a difference between them. This is typically accomplished by compressing anywhere from 2 to 6 dB or so at anywhere from a 2:1 to 8:1 ratio, although some situations may require more radical settings.

Setting the Compressor

The timing of the attack and release is important, so here are a few steps to setting up those parameters in your compressor. One of the easiest ways to do that is to use the snare drum as your template, assuming that you're mixing a song with a more or less constant tempo. You can then use the same approximate attack and release settings for the other instruments. *The idea is to make the compressor breathe in time with the song.*

1. Start with the attack time set as slow as possible, and release time set as fast as possible on the compressor.

2. Turn the attack faster until the instrument (in this case, the snare) begins to sound dull (this happens because you're compressing the attack portion of the sound envelope). Stop increasing the attack time at this point and even back it off a little.

3. Adjust the release time so that after the snare hits, the volume goes back to 90 to 100 percent normal by the next snare beat.

4. Add the rest of the mix back in and listen. Make slight adjustments to the attack and release times as needed.

How Much Compression Do I Need?

How much compression you use is a matter of taste. That being said, the more compression you use, the more likely that you'll hear it working. Generally speaking, compression of 6 dB or less is used more for controlling dynamics than for imparting any sonic quality, but it's also common to see as much as 15 or even 20 dB used for electric guitars, room mics, drums, and even vocals, depending upon the situation. In the final analysis, the amount of compression depends on the song, the arrangement, the player, the room, the instrument or vocalist, or the sound you're looking for.

Compression As An Effect

Compression is interesting because of how much it can change the sound of a track under the right circumstances. Sometimes it can make a track seem closer to the listener, or seem more aggressive and exciting. The attack and release controls can modify the volume envelope of a sound to have more or less attack or release, which can make it sound punchy or fatter, or make a note have a longer decay.

Sometimes massive amounts of compression (like 15 or 20 dB) can impart a sound into the track that you can't get any other way, and sometimes even a dB or two can change the sound of a track just enough to get you where you want to go.

Limiting

While a compressor increases the low level and decreases the loud ones to even out the dynamic range, a limiter keeps the level from ever going much louder once it hits the threshold. It's very much like a truck with a speed governor on it that keeps the truck at 60 mph regardless of how much more you press down on the gas pedal. With a limiter, once you hit the predetermined signal level, it never gets much louder no matter how much more input level it receives.

A compressor and a limiter are somewhat the same except for the settings. Any time the compression ratio is set to 10:1 or more, it's considered a limiter. Limiting is usually used in sound reinforcement for speaker protection (there are some limiters on powered studio monitors as well), and not used much in mixing with the following exception.

Most modern digital limiters (either hardware or software) have a function known as "look ahead" which allows the detector circuitry to look at the signal a millisecond or two before it hits the limiter.

Figure 6.7: The T-RackS Brickwall Limiter

This means that the limiter acts extremely fast and just about eliminates any overshoot of the predetermined level, which can be a problem with analog limiters. See Figure 6.7 for an example of a digital limiter with a look-ahead function.

Many engineers who feel that the bass guitar is the anchor for the song want the bass to have as little dynamic range as possible. This can be achieved by limiting the bass by 3 to 6 dB (depending on the song) with a ratio of 10:1, 20:1 or even higher.

Compressing The Various Instruments

Most instruments can benefit from a least some compression, either for the purpose of smoothing out a performance, raising or lowering a note or drum hit that might be getting lost or is too loud, or as an effect. Let's look at how it works on the most commonly used instruments.

Compressing The Drums

There are a number of reasons to compress the drums. Sometimes a drummer doesn't hit every beat on the kick and snare with the same intensity, which makes the pulse of the song erratic. Sometimes the toms fills have different volumes across the drums. And in terms of effects, compression does work wonders to push the kick and snare forward in the track to make them much more punchy. Let's do some experimenting.

Exercise Pod - Compressing The Drums

Using the setup and tracks from the previous chapter, insert a compressor on any insert of the snare drum channel. We'll choose the snare drum first because it's usually easy to hear how the compressor is affecting it. To begin, set the *Threshold* control so that no compression occurs, the *Ratio* set at 2:1, and the *Attack* and *Release* controls and the *Output* control set to mid-way.

E6.1: Compressing The Snare

A) Solo the snare, then slowly decrease the *Threshold* until the *Gain Reduction Meter* reads 2 dB. Can you hear the compression? What does the master mix bus meter read? Can you hear a difference if you bypass the compressor?

B) Increase the *Threshold* until the *Gain Reduction Meter* reads 10 dB. Can you hear the compression? What does the master mix bus meter read now? Can you hear a difference if you bypass the compressor?

C) Return the *Threshold* control to where there's only 2 dB of gain reduction. Now increase the Ratio control from 2:1 to 6:1. What does the gain reduction meter read now? What does the master mix bus meter read now? Can you hear the compression? Can you hear a difference if you bypass the compressor?

D) Now increase the *Ratio* control from 2:1 to 20:1. What does the gain reduction meter read now? What does the master mix bus meter read now? Can you hear the compression? Can you hear the difference if you bypass the compressor?

E) Return the *Ratio* control to 4:1 and increase the *Threshold* control until there's about 3 dB of gain reduction occurring. Now decrease the *Attack* time to as fast as it will go. What does the gain reduction meter read now? What does the master mix bus meter read now? Can you hear the compression? Can you hear the difference if you bypass the compressor?

F) Increase the *Attack* time to its slowest setting. What does the gain reduction meter read now? What does the master mix bus meter read now? Can you hear the compression? Can you hear the difference if you bypass the compressor?

G) Now decrease the *Attack* time until the sound of the snare just begins to dull. What does the gain reduction meter read now? What does the master mix bus meter read now? Can you hear the compression? Can you hear the difference if you bypass the compressor?

H) Increase the *Release* time to as slow as it will go. What does the gain reduction meter read now? What does the master mix bus meter read now? Can you hear the compression? Can you hear the difference if you bypass the compressor?

I) Decrease the *Release* time to as fast as it will go. What does the gain reduction meter read now? What does the master mix bus meter read now? Can you hear the compression? Can you hear the difference if you bypass the compressor?

J) Increase the *Release* time until the snare reaches 90 to 100 percent volume on the next snare hit. What does the gain reduction meter read now? What does the master mix bus meter read now? Can you hear the compression? Can you hear the difference if you bypass the compressor?

K) Select the *Bypass* to hear the volume of the snare without the compressor. Now deselect the Bypass and slowly raise the *Output* control until the compressed signal level is equal to the uncompressed signal in level. Continue to use the *Bypass* to check.

L) Un-solo the snare track and listen to it with the rest of the mix. What do you notice about the snare? Can you hear the compression? What does the master mix bus meter read now?

M) To make the snare seem closer to you in the mix, increase the compression by increasing the *Threshold* or *Ratio* controls.

E6.2: Compressing The Kick

A) Solo the kick and follow the same procedure as A through F in E6.1 to hear the extreme effects of the parameter settings.

B) Set the *Attack* time as slow as it will go, then increase it until the sound of the kick just begins to dull. What does the gain reduction meter read now? What does the master mix bus meter read now? Can you hear the compression? Can you hear the difference if you bypass the compressor?

C) Now increase the *Release* time to as slow as it will go and increase it until the kick reaches 90 to 100 percent volume on the next snare hit. What does the gain reduction meter read now? What does the master mix bus meter read now? Can you hear the compression? Can you hear the difference if you bypass the compressor?

D) Select the *Bypass* to hear the volume of the kick without the compressor. Now deselect the Bypass and slowly raise the *Output* control until the compressed signal is equal to the uncompressed signal in level. Continue to use the *Bypass* to check.

E) Un-solo the kick track and listen to it with the rest of the mix. What do you notice about the kick? Can you hear the compression? What does the master mix bus meter read now?

F) To make the kick seem closer to you in the mix, increase the compression by increasing the *Threshold* or *Ratio* controls.

E6.3: Compressing The Toms

Go to a place in the song that has a tom fill and set the DAW to loop at that point.

A) Solo the toms and follow the same procedure as A through F in E6.1 to hear the extreme effects of the parameter settings.

B) Set the *Attack* time as slow as it will go, then increase it until the sound of the toms just begins to dull. What does the gain reduction meter read now? What does the master mix bus meter read now? Can you hear the compression? Can you hear the difference if you bypass the compressor?

C) Use the same release time as used on the snare, or increase the release time to as slow as it will go and increase it until the one hit reaches 90 to 100 percent volume on the next tom hit. What does the gain reduction meter read now? What does the master mix bus meter read now? Can you hear the compression? Can you hear the difference if you bypass the compressor?

D) Select the *Bypass* to hear the volume of the toms without the compressor. Now deselect the Bypass and slowly raise the *Output* control until the compressed signal is equal to the uncompressed signal in level. Continue to use the *Bypass* to check.

E) Un-solo the tom tracks and listen to it with the rest of the mix. What do you notice about the toms? Can you hear the compression? What does the master mix bus meter read now?

F) To make the toms seem closer to you in the mix, increase the compression by increasing the *Threshold* or *Ratio* controls.

E6.4: Compressing The Room Mics

A) Solo the room mics and follow the same procedure as A through F in E6.1 to hear the extreme effects of the parameter settings.

B) Set the *Attack* time as slow as it will go, then increase it until the sound of the room just begins to dull. What does the gain reduction meter read now? What does the master mix bus meter read now? Can you hear the compression? Can you hear the difference if you bypass the compressor?

C) Now increase the *Release* time to as slow as it will go and increase it until the room reaches 90 to 100 percent volume on the next snare hit. What does the gain reduction meter read now? What does the master mix bus meter read now? Can you hear the compression? Can you hear the difference if you bypass the compressor?

D) Select the *Bypass* to hear the volume of the room without the compressor. Now deselect the *Bypass* and slowly raise the *Output* control until the compressed signal is equal to the uncompressed signal in level. Continue to use the *Bypass* to check.

E) Un-solo the room tracks and listen to them with the rest of the mix. What do you notice about the room? Can you hear the compression? What does the master mix bus meter read now?

F) Many mixers prefer the room sound to be extremely compressed because of the unique sound that imparts. Increase the compression by increasing the *Threshold* or *Ratio* controls until there's about 10 dB or more of compression, then tuck the room tracks in just under the other drum tracks. What do you notice about the drum sound? What does the master mix bus meter read now?

E6.5: Compressing The Entire Kit

A) Insert a compressor into the subgroup signal path so it will affect the entire drum kit.

B) Set the compressor so there's about 2 dB of gain reduction.

C) Set the *Attack* time as slow as it will go, then increase it until the sound of the kit just begins to dull. What does the gain reduction meter read now? What does the master mix bus meter read now? Can you hear the compression? Can you hear the difference if you bypass the compressor? What does it do to the cymbals?

D) Now increase the *Release* time to as slow as it will go and increase it until the room reaches 90 to 100 percent volume on the next snare hit. What does the gain reduction meter read now? What does the master mix bus meter read now? Can you hear the compression? Can you hear the difference if you bypass the compressor? What do the cymbals sound like?

E) Select the *Bypass* to hear the volume of the room without the compressor. Now deselect the *Bypass* and slowly raise the *Output* control until the compressed signal is equal to the uncompressed signal in level. Continue to use the *Bypass* to check.

F) Increase the compression by increasing the *Threshold* or *Ratio* controls. What does the gain reduction meter read now? What does the master mix bus meter read now? Can you hear the compression? Can you hear the difference if you bypass the compressor? What do the cymbals sound like?

G) Bypass the subgroup drum compressor.

Parallel Compression

There's a great trick that really punches up the drum sound without adding more compression to the individual tracks. It's something I call the "The New York Compression Trick" because when I was starting out, every mixer in New York used it on their mixes. Now everyone uses it so it's not that exclusive to New York City any more, so we'll just call it by its more academic name — parallel compression.

Essentially the trick centers around an additional drum subgroup that has a compressor with some rather extreme settings. Once the subgroup is set up and the compressor is kicking, the subgroup is gently raised until it's just barely heard against the original drum mix. If you want the drums punchier, just add more subgroup level.

Be warned — the sound that you get out of the drums when using parallel compression is addicting, and you'll want to use it on every mix (which is perfectly okay if it works for you).

E6.6: Parallel Compression On The Drums

A) Assign the drums to a separate subgroup. If you're already bused to one, use a second.

B) Insert a stereo compressor to the subgroup and set it so there's about 10 dB of compression and the *Attack* and *Release* so it breathes with the track.

C) Raise the fader level of the subgroup with the compressor until it's tucked just under the present rhythm section mix to where you can just hear it. Does it sound punchier? What does the master mix bus meter read?

D) For an even greater effect, EQ the subgroup with +10 dB at 10kHz and +10 dB at 100Hz. What does it sound like now?

E) Add the bass guitar to the new subgroup mix. What does it sound like now?

Compressing The Bass

Most basses inherently have notes that are louder or softer than others depending upon where they're played on the neck of the instrument. This is especially noticeable on a bass played with a pick instead of fingers. Some notes just roar while others might get lost, which is why at least some compression is usually necessary on the instrument. On the other hand, there are some mixers that build their mixes around the bass and want the level to be virtually the same throughout the song, so they'll set the compressor accordingly.

The *Ratio* control is important to dialing in the right amount of compression on the bass. Watch the channel meter, and if there are a lot of wild peaks, a higher ratio and higher threshold, which provides less compression, is required. If you just want to round out the sound, use a lower compression ratio and a lower threshold for more compression.

Exercise Pod - Compressing The Bass

E6.7: Solo the bass. If there are direct and amp tracks and they're sub-grouped, then solo the subgroup and insert a compressor in the subgroup signal path.

A) Set the *Ratio* at 4:1 and adjust the *Threshold* so that there's about 2 dB of compression. Did the sound of the bass change? Are the notes more even? Can you hear the compression? What happens to the master mix bus meters?

B) Increase the *Threshold* until the *Gain Reduction Meter* reads 10 dB. Can you hear the compression? What does the master mix bus meter read now? Can you hear the difference if you bypass the compressor?

C) Return the *Threshold* control to where there's only 2 dB of gain reduction. Now increase the Ratio control from 4:1 to 12:1. What does the gain reduction meter read now? What does the master mix bus meter read now? Can you hear the compression? Can you hear the difference if you bypass the compressor? Does the bass sound more even or does it sound choked?

D) Return the *Ratio* control to 4:1 and increase the *Threshold* control until there's about 3 dB of gain reduction occurring. Now decrease the Attack time to as fast as it will go. What does the gain reduction meter read now? What does the master mix bus meter read now? Can you hear the compression? Can you hear the difference if you bypass the compressor? Does the bass sound better or worse?

E) Increase the *Attack* time to as slow as it will go. What does the gain reduction meter read now? What does the master mix bus meter read now? Can you hear the compression? Can you hear the difference if you bypass the compressor? Does the bass sound better or worse?

F) Now decrease the *Attack* time until the sound of the bass just begins to dull. What does the gain reduction meter read now? What does the master mix bus meter read now? Can you hear the compression? Can you hear the difference if you bypass the compressor? Does the bass sound better or worse?

G) Increase the *Release* time to its slowest setting. What does the gain reduction meter read now? What does the master mix bus meter read now? Can you hear the compression? Can you hear the difference if you bypass the compressor?

H) Decrease the *Release* time to its fastest setting. What does the gain reduction meter read now? What does the master mix bus meter read now? Can you hear the compression? Can you hear the difference if you bypass the compressor? Does the bass sound better or worse?

I) Increase the *Release* time until the bass breathes with the track or the notes feel longer, or set it to the approximate *Release* setting of the snare compressor. What does the gain reduction meter read now? What does the master mix bus meter read now? Can you hear the compression? Can you hear the difference if you bypass the compressor?

J) Select the *Bypass* to hear the volume of the bass without the compressor. Now deselect the Bypass and slowly raise the *Output* control until the compressed signal is equal to the uncompressed signal in level. Continue to use the *Bypass* to check.

K) Un-solo the bass track or subgroup and listen to it with the rest of the mix. What do you notice about the bass? Can you hear the compression? What does the master mix bus meter read now?

L) Many mixers prefer that the bass have no dynamics in order to keep the mix solid and punchy. To accomplish this, increase *Ratio* control to 12:1 or more and increase the *Threshold* until there is between 3 and 6 dB of compression.

The settings for a miked bass amp might be different, depending upon how distorted it is.

Compressing Guitars

Clean electric guitars and acoustic guitars can greatly benefit from compression, but distorted guitars are already naturally compressed. That being said, a little extra compression can make a lead guitar stand out from a track.

Acoustic and clean electric guitars generally have the a lot dynamic range and usually require more compression. Direct clean guitars require the most, sometimes 10 dB or more. With a guitar that's amplified, usually the more distorted it becomes, the less compression it requires, although most electric guitars usually require at least a few dB.

As with the bass, the ratio control is important to dialing in the right amount of compression. Watch the meter and if there are a lot of wild peaks, a higher ratio and higher threshold is required. If you just want to round out the sound, use a lower compression ratio and a lower threshold, which will give you more compression.

Exercise Pod - Compressing Electric Guitars

E6.8: A) Solo the electric guitar. If there are a lot of peaks as you watch the meter, set the *Ratio* at about 8:1 and the *Threshold* to where there's about 2 dB of compression. If there aren't any peaks, set the *ratio* at about 4:1 and the *threshold* to where there's about 4 dB of compression. What does it sound like? Can you hear the compression?

B) Set the *Attack* and *Release* controls as described previously to breathe with the track, but also experiment with extreme settings. What does it sound like with the *Attack* set as long as possible? What does it sound like with the *Release* set as long as possible? What does it sound like with the *Attack* set as short as possible? What does it sound like with the *Release* set as short as possible?

C) Bypass the compressor and listen to the level. Does it need any make-up gain? Add as needed.

D) With the attack and release set, unsolo the electric guitar. What does it sound like in the track? Is it more or less present? Can you hear it better? Does the channel level need adjusting?

Exercise Pod - Compressing The Acoustic Guitar

Although there's not an acoustic guitar on the examples on the DVD, try this exercise if one of your songs has one.

E6.9: A) Solo the acoustic guitar. If there are a lot of peaks as you watch the meter, set the *Ratio* at about 8:1 and the *Threshold* to where there's about 2 dB of compression. If there aren't any peaks, set the *Ratio* at about 4:1 and the *Threshold* to where there's about 4 dB of compression. What does it sound like? Can you hear the compression?

B) Set the *Attack* and *Release* controls as described previously to breathe with the track, but also experiment with extreme settings. What does it sound like with the *Attack* set as long as possible? What does it sound like with the *Release* set as long as possible? What does it sound like with the *Attack* set as short as possible? What does it sound like with the *Release* set as short as possible?

C) Bypass the compressor and listen to the level. Does it need any make-up gain? Add as needed.

D) With the attack and release set, un-solo the acoustic guitar. What does it sound like in the track? Is it more or less present? Can you hear it better? Does the channel level need adjusting?

Compressing Keyboards

Like guitars, compression on keyboards depends on how wild the dynamic swings are. An acoustic piano is inherently much more dynamic than a synthesizer or organ, so it must be treated differently as a result.

Sampled acoustic or electric pianos don't have nearly the dynamic range of a real acoustic instrument, but they still can have some major peaks depending upon the way they're played. Beware that the more compression used, the less realistic an acoustic piano sounds.

Sometimes organ and string sounds, which aren't very dynamic, can benefit from a touch of compression to make sure all the notes are heard evenly, which pulls them in front of the mix a bit.

Exercise Pod - Compressing Keyboards

E6.10: A) Solo the keyboard. If there are a lot of peaks as you watch the meter, set the *Ratio* at about 8:1 and the *Threshold* to where there's about 2 dB of compression. If there aren't any peaks, set the Ratio at about 4:1 and the *Threshold* to where there's about 4 dB of compression. What does it sound like? Can you hear the compression?

B) Set the *Attack* and *Release* controls as described previously to breathe with the track, but also experiment with extreme settings. What does it sound like with the *Attack* set as long as possible? What does it sound like with the *Release* set as long as possible? What does it sound like with the *Attack* set as short as possible? What does it sound like with the *Release* set as short as possible?

C) Bypass the compressor and listen to the level. Does it need any make-up gain? Add as needed.

D) With the attack and release set, un-solo the keyboard. What does it sound like in the track? Is it more or less present? Can you hear it better? Does the channel level need adjusting?

Compressing Vocals

If there's one instrument that greatly benefits from compression it's the human voice. Most singers aren't able to sing every word or line at the same level, so some words get buried as a result. Compression evens out the level differences so you can better hear every word.

The amount of compression can vary wildly on a vocal if it has a lot of dynamic range, with a whisper to a scream within the same song, so it's not uncommon to use as much as 10 dB or more on some vocals.

Exercise Pod - Compressing The Lead Vocal

E6.11: A) Solo the lead vocal. If there are a lot of peaks as you watch the meter, set the *Ratio* at about 8:1 and the *Threshold* to where there's about 2 dB of compression. If there aren't any peaks, set the *Ratio* at about 4:1 and the *Threshold* to where there's about 4 dB of compression. What does it sound like? Can you hear the compression?

B) Set the *Attack* and *Release* controls as described previously to breathe with the track, but also experiment with extreme settings. What does it sound like with the *Attack* set as long as possible? What does it sound like with the *Release* set as long as possible? What does it sound like with the Attack set as short as possible? What does it sound like with the *Release* set as short as possible?

C) Bypass the compressor and listen to the level. Does it need any make-up gain? Add as needed.

D) With the attack and release set, un-solo the lead vocal. What does it sound like in the track? Is it more or less present? Can you hear it better? Does the channel level need adjusting?

E) Increase the compression. Does the vocal come out front more? Does it sound too compressed or choked?

Compressing Other Instruments

The principles of compressing other instruments are identical to any of the above instruments, so let's review.

- Acoustic instruments are usually more dynamic than electric instruments, and therefore need to be controlled more.

- The more wild the peaks, the higher the compression ratio should be. The fewer the peaks, the lower the ratio.

- The more compression you use, the more likely that you'll hear it and color the sound.

- If you set the attack and release times of the compressor so it breathes with the track, the less likely you'll hear it working in the track.

Compressing Loops

Care should be taken when compressing loops or samples as these are usually heavily compressed already. One of the byproducts of additional compression is to change the groove, which won't be desirable in most cases. Sometimes just a few dB of limiting can handle the peaks and allow it to sit better in the mix.

Figure 6.8: A Typical de-esser

Exercise Pod - Compressing Loops

Open Example 4 on the DVD for a song with loops.

E6.12: Solo the loop. Set the *Ratio* at about 2:1 and the *Threshold* to where there's about 2 dB of compression. Set the *Attack* and *Release* controls to breathe with the track. What does it sound like? Un-solo it and see how it fits in the track? Can you hear the compression? Does the groove change?

E6.13: Increase the compression to 10 dB. What does it sound like? Un-solo it and see how it fits in the track? Can you hear the compression? Does the groove change?

E6.14: Set the *Ratio* at about 12:1 and the *Threshold* to where there's about 2 dB of compression. What does it sound like? Un-solo it and see how it fits in the track? Can you hear the compression? Does the groove change?

E6.15: Increase the compression to 10 dB. What does it sound like? Un-solo it and see how it fits in the track? Can you hear the compression? Does the groove change?

E6.16: Set the *Ratio* and the amount of compression that seems to work best with track and balance it accordingly.

De-essers

Sometimes a vocal has a short bursts of high-frequency energy where the "s" sounds are over-emphasized, which is known as "sibilance." It comes from a combination of mic technique by the vocalist, the type of mic used, and heavy compression on the vocal track. Sibilance is nasty sounding and generally felt to be highly undesirable, so a special type of compressor called a de-esser is used to counteract it (see Figure 6.8). A de-esser can be tuned to compress only a selected band of frequencies between 3 and 10kHz to eliminate sibilance.

Most de-essers have only two controls; *Threshold* and *Frequency*. Some have a *Listen* button that allow you to solo only the frequency that's being compressed, which can be helpful in finding the offending frequency.

If you have a de-esser or de-esser plug-in, try the following exercise.

Exercise Pod - Using The De-esser

E6.17: Solo the lead vocal and insert the de-esser on the channel.

A) Raise the *Threshold* control until the sibilance is decreased, but so you can still hear the "S's". If you can't hear them, then you've raised the *Threshold* too far.

B) Span the available frequencies with the *Frequency* control until you find the one that's most offensive.

C) Un-solo the vocal and listen in context with the track. Is the sound the vocal natural? Is there any remaining sibilance? Can you distinguish the "s" sounds?

Gates

A gate (sometimes called a "noise gate" or "expander") is sort of a reverse-compressor. That is, it works backwards from a normal compressor in that the sound level is at its loudest until it reaches the threshold, where it's then decreased or muted completely.

A gate can be used to cover up noises, buzzes, coughs or other low level noises that were recorded on a track. For example, a gate can be used on electric guitar tracks to effectively eliminate amplifier noise when the guitar player isn't playing. On drums, gates can be used to turn off the leakage from the tom mics, since they tend to muddy up the other drum tracks.

Figure 6.9: A Typical Noise Gate

Like the de-esser, a gate can sometimes consist of just a few controls, principally the *threshold, range* and sometimes *hold* or *release* controls (see Figure 6.9). *Range* sets the amount of attenuation after the threshold is reached and the gate turns on. Sometimes when gating drums, the *Range* control is set so it attenuates the signal only about 10 or 20 dB. This lets some of the natural ambience remain and prevents the drums from sounding choked. The *hold* control keeps the gate open a defined amount of time, and the release control works just like on a compressor.

Exercise Pod - Using A Gate

E6.18: Using a Gate on Electric Guitar

A) Solo the electric guitar and insert the gate on the channel. Then go to a place in the track where there's amplifier noise just before the guitar plays.

B) Raise the *Threshold* control until the noise is decreased, then move to a place where the guitar is playing. If the gate is still on and you can't hear the guitar, then you've raised the *Threshold* too far. Back it off until you can hear the guitar again, then go back to the noisy part and see if you can still hear it.

C) Sometimes a gate will switch quickly between its on and off states depending on how the controls (mostly the *Threshold*) are set. If that's the case, try fine-tuning the settings of the *Threshold* and *Release* controls (if the gate has one). If it still chatters, add a compressor before the gate to keep the signal steady.

E6.19: Using a Gate on the Snare Drum

A) Solo the snare and insert the gate on the channel.

B) Raise the *Threshold* control until you can hear the snare drum hit, but no sound in between hits. Un-solo the track. Does it sound natural? Does it sound cut off?

C) Adjust the *Range* control so the snare is attenuated by 10 dB between hits. Does it sound natural? Does it sound cut off?

D) If the gate chatters, try fine tuning the settings of the *Threshold* and *Release* controls (if the gate has one). If it still chatters, add a compressor before the gate to keep the signal steady. Refer to Example 3 on the DVD.

E6.20: Using a Gate on the Toms

A) Go to a place in the song where there's a tom fill. Solo the tom and insert the gate on the channel.

B) Raise the *Threshold* control until you can hear the tom drum hit, but no sound in between hits. Un-solo the track. Does it sound natural? Does it sound cut off?

C) Adjust the *Range* control so the tom is attenuated by 10 dB between hits. Does it sound natural? Does it sound cut off?

D) If the gate chatters, try fine tuning the settings of the *Threshold* and *Release* controls (if the gate has one). If it still chatters, add a compressor before the gate to keep the signal steady.

CHAPTER 7
USING THE EQ

No part of mixing draws more questions that adding EQ. Where do I do it? How much is enough? What frequencies do I use? Is it okay if I don't use any? These are all legitimate questions that many beginning mixers have that will be answered as this chapter goes along.

Equalization Basics

Before you begin twisting equalizer knobs, it helps to understand the situations where EQing might be necessary, since there are more than one. They are:

- To make an instrument sound clearer and more defined.

- To make the instrument sound bigger and larger than life.

- To make all the elements of a mix fit better together.

It's all too common for someone new to mixing to solo a track, grab the EQ, and endlessly search for what seems to be the right sound. The only problem is that you don't know what the right sound really is unless you listen to everything else in the mix together. If you keep these three goals in mind, you'll avoid a lot of indiscriminate knob twirling and endless

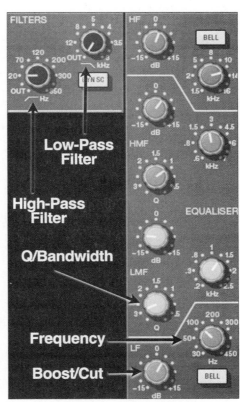

Figure 7.1: The Controls Of A Typical Equalizer

searching for the right setting. And remember, there's no rule that says you have to use the EQ at all if the track sounds good and works with the other tracks already.

EQ Parameters

There are a number of parameters that you'll find on most equalizers (see Figure 7.1).

Frequency: The *Frequency* control selects the center frequency around which the equalizer operates, and comes in many forms. It can be a fixed frequency like the tone controls on a car radio or guitar amplifier, a selectable frequency where a button or detent selects the frequency, or a variable or swept frequency control where you can continuously select the frequency that's appropriate.

Boost/Cut: This is the control that adds or subtracts the volume of the particular frequency, or band of frequencies chosen.

Q, Bandwidth: This control selects the band of frequencies that the equalizer will boost or cut. A Q set on 10 will only affect a narrow number of frequencies around the frequency selected, so it's very precise and excellent for cutting an offensive frequency spike. A Q of 2 affects several octaves above and below the center frequency (if 1,000 is selected, it may affect everything from 500Hz through 2,000Hz). The Q or *bandwidth* control is not found on all equalizers.

High-Pass Filter, Low-Cut: The high-pass filter (sometimes abbreviated with HPF) allows high frequencies to pass and cuts off low frequencies. Sometimes the HPF (also sometimes more appropriately called *low-cut* because the low frequencies are filtered) has a fixed frequency like at 40 or 60Hz, sometimes there are several frequencies that are selectable, and sometimes the frequency selection is continuously variable.

Low-Pass Filter, High-Cut: The low-pass filter (sometimes abbreviated with LPF) allows low frequencies to pass and cuts off high frequencies. Sometimes HPF (also sometimes more appropriately called *high-cut* because the high frequencies are filtered) has a fixed frequency like 10kHz or 12kHz, sometimes there are several frequencies that are selectable, and sometimes the frequency selection is continuously variable.

In/Out: *In* inserts the equalizer into the circuit while *Out* bypasses it.

A Description Of The Audio Bands

The audio bandwidth is made up of six distinct frequency bands. Each one has an enormous impact on the final sound, so it's important to know the characteristics of each before we begin to use the equalizer.

Frequency Band	Description	Consequences
Sub Bass **16Hz to 60Hz**	Sounds that are often felt more than heard. They give the music a sense of power	Too much emphasis in this range makes the music sound muddy. Attenuating this range (especially below 40kHz) can clean a mix up considerably.

Frequency Band	Description	Consequences
Bass **60Hz to 250Hz**	Contains the fundamental notes of the rhythm section	EQing this range can make the musical balance either fat or thin. Too much boost in this range can make the music sound boomy.
Low Mids **250Hz to 2kHz**	Contains the low harmonics of most musical instruments	Can introduce a telephone-like quality to the music if boosted too much. Boosting the 500 to 1000Hz octave makes the instruments sound horn-like. Boosting the 1 to 2kHz octave makes them sound tinny. Excess output in this range can cause listening fatigue.
High Mids **2k to 4kHz**	Controls the speech recognition sounds of m, b and v	Too much boost in this range, especially at 3kHz, can introduce a lisping quality to a voice. Too much boost in this range can cause listening fatigue. Dipping the 3kHz range on instrument backgrounds and slightly peaking 3kHz on vocals can make the vocals audible without having to decrease the instrumental level in mixes where the voice would otherwise seem buried.
Presence **4k to 6kHz**	Responsible for the clarity and definition of voices and instruments	Boosting this range can make the music seem closer to the listener. Reducing the 5kHz content of a mix makes the sound more distant and transparent.
Brilliance **6k to 16kHz**	Controls the brilliance and clarity of sounds	Too much emphasis in this range can produce sibilance on the vocals.

Figure 7.2: Audio Band Description

Using The Equalizer

There are many different methods for EQing an instrument or vocal, but here are a couple of tried and true techniques that will never steer you wrong.

Subtractive Equalization

While it's natural to believe that by adding some EQ here and there that you'll make the instrument or vocal sound better, that's not necessarily the case. There's a very effective EQ technique called "subtractive equalization" that works by attenuating frequencies instead of boosting them. Many superstar mixers love this method because it makes the sound of the track more natural than if you boosted any of the frequencies. This is because every time you boost an EQ, there's a slight amount of something called phase shift that's added to the signal as a byproduct of the way an electronic equalizer works. By using subtractive equalization, you completely avoid this artifact. As a result, the track is better able to blend with the others.

Here's how to use subtractive equalization:

1. Set the *Boost/Cut* control to a moderate level of cut (8 or 10 dB should work.)

2. Sweep through the frequencies until you find the frequency where the sound has the least amount of boxiness and the most definition.

3. Adjust the amount of cut to taste. Be aware that too much cut makes the sound thinner.

Alternately you can try a different approach.

1. Set the *Boost/Cut* control to a moderate level of boost (8 or 10 dB should work.)

2. Sweep through the frequencies until you find the frequency that really leaps out above all others. That's the frequency to cut.

3. Adjust the amount of cut to taste. Be aware that too much cut makes the sound thinner.

There are two frequency ranges that are particularly effective when using subtractive equalization; from 400 to 600Hz and between 2kHz and 4kHz. The reason why 400 to 600Hz is chosen is because most directional microphones provide a natural boost in that frequency range because of the *proximity effect* that results from miking an instrument or voice up close. Likewise, many mics that are known as good vocal mics have a presence boost between 2kHz and 4kHz. Cutting those frequencies a few dB (more or less as needed) can make the track sound much more natural than if you were to try to boost other frequencies instead.

These two problem areas usually crop up when you're recording everything with the same microphone, since there's a buildup in the frequency areas as more and more instruments are recorded. By cutting a few dB from these frequency ranges you'll find that the instruments sit better in the mix without ever having to add as much EQ.

Sometimes you want to be sure that the instrument has a lot of definition. To do that, you can go a few steps further:

4. Add some "point" to the sound by adding a slight amount (start with only 1 dB, then add more to taste) of upper midrange (1k to 4kHz).

5. If required, add some "sparkle" to sound by adding a slight amount of high frequencies (4kHz to 10kHz).

6. If required, add some "air" to sound by adding a slight amount of the brilliance frequencies (10kHz to 15kHz).

Juggling Frequencies

One of the biggest problems during mixing is when two instruments clash because their predominant frequencies are in the same bandwidth. This often happens with two similar guitars in the mix (like if they're both Strats played through Marshalls), but lots of other combinations, like between a guitar and a lead vocal, or a snare drum and a guitar, happen as well. The way to avoid this is to use a method called "juggling frequencies."

Veteran engineers know that soloing a track then equalizing it without listening to any of the other tracks at the same time inevitably causes a frequency clash between the EQed track and another track in the mix. The way to avoid this is to listen to other instruments while you're EQing, and when you find two instruments that have frequencies that clash, solo only those. Here's how it's done.

Make sure that the equalizers of the two offending channels are not boosting at the same frequency. If they are, move one to a slightly higher or lower frequency.

If an instrument's equalizer is cutting at a certain frequency, boost the frequency of the other instrument at that same frequency. For example, if the kick is cut at 500Hz, boost the bass at 500Hz.

Also, you'll probably have to do a lot of back-and-forth EQing where you start with one instrument, then tweak another that's clashing, then return to the original one, and back again over and over until each one can be heard distinctly.

Remember that after frequency juggling, an instrument might sound terrible when soloed by itself. That's okay, because the idea is for it to work well in the track with the rest of the instruments.

The Magic High-Pass Filter

One of the most useful and overlooked equalization parameters available to a mixer is the high-pass filter (HPF). The high-pass filter can be another parameter on an equalizer, or it can be a stand-alone plug-in or device. The HPF does just what it says; it allows high frequencies to pass and cuts off low frequencies.

The low frequencies of many instruments sometimes just clash with each other and in the end, don't add much to the sound anyway. That's why if you roll the low frequencies off below 100 or even 150Hz on most instruments other than the kick and bass, the mix begins to clean up almost magically.

For instance, by rolling off the low frequencies of a vocal mic, you can eliminate the rumble of trucks and machinery that you can't physically hear because they're so low, yet they can muddy up the mix. Rolling off the low end of an electric guitar keeps it out of the way of the rhythm section and helps it to fit better the mix. Even rolling off the bass and drums anywhere in between 40 and 60Hz can sometimes make the mix both louder and punchier without any sense of losing the low end.

The Principles of Equalization

Here are some general equalization principles that can speed up the EQ process and keep you from chasing your EQ tail.

- The fewer instruments that are in the mix, the bigger each one should sound.

- Conversely, the more instruments in the mix, the smaller each one needs to be for everything to fit together.

- If it sounds muddy, cut some at 250Hz.

- If it sounds honky, cut some at 500Hz.

- Cut if you're trying to make things sound clearer.

- Boost if you're trying to make things sound different.

- You can't boost something that's not there in the first place.

- Use a narrow Q or bandwidth when cutting (like somewhere between 6 and 10), and a wide Q (like between .5 and 2) when boosting

- If you want something to stick out, roll off the bottom; if you want it to blend in, roll off the top

EQing Various Instruments

While many engineers have certain frequencies that they either like or don't like, it's much easier to get everything to fit together in a mix if you realize that every mix is different. The song is different, the players are different, the instruments might be different, the arrangement is different, and a whole host of other things that truly make each one unique. That's what we both love and hate about music. It's not a cookie-cutter operation at all, although you'll find that each class of instrument may have certain frequency ranges that work a little more than others.

Let's look at equalizing some commonly used instruments.

Equalizing The Drums

The drums present an interesting dilemma: does the song demand that the drum kit work as a whole, or should the snare or kick stand out? Once again, it depends upon the song, but we can take a look at both approaches.

The kick and snare are extremely important in modern music because the kick is the heartbeat and the snare drives the song. By simply getting the sound and balance of these two drums right, it's possible to change a song from dull to exciting.

There are certain frequencies on different drums that you should be aware of.

Kick: Bottom at 80 to 100Hz, hollowness at 400Hz, point at 3 to 5kHz

Snare: Fatness at 120 to 240Hz, point at 900Hz, crispness at 5kHz, snap at 10kHz

Hat: Clang at 200Hz, sparkle at 8 to 10kHz

Rack Toms: Fullness at 240 to 500Hz, attack at 5 to 7kHz

Floor Tom: Fullness at 80Hz, attack at 5kHz

Cymbals: Clang at 200Hz, sparkle at 8 to 10kHz

These frequencies are not cut and dried for each drum kit, since the size of the drum or cymbal and the material they're made of contributes greatly to the tone. Remember to sweep the frequencies around each of the above to find the correct frequency for that particular drum or cymbal.

Beware that boosting from 40 to 60Hz may make the kick sound big on your speakers, but it might not be heard when played back on smaller speakers. Also remember that the ideal spot for a 22-inch kick drum (which is the most commonly used) is around 80Hz.

Exercise Pod - EQing The Drums
E7.1: EQing The Snare

Use the mix that you previously built in Chapter 6. Begin by soloing the entire drum kit either individually or via the group or subgroup.

A) Can you hear the snare distinctly? Is it crisp and full sounding, or thin and dull?

B) Add 2 dB at 1kHz. Does it come forward in the mix? Does it sound tinny?

C) Cut 2 dB at 1kHz. Does it blend better in the mix? Did it lose its presence?

D) Add 2 dB at 5kHz. Does it come forward in the mix? Does it sound tinny or too bright?

E) Cut 2 dB at 5kHz. Does it blend better in the mix? Did it lose its presence?

F) Add 2 dB at 10kHz. Does it come forward in the mix? Does it sound tinny? Does it have more snap?

G) Cut 2 dB at 10kHz. Does it blend better in the mix? Did it lose its presence?

H) Add 2 dB at 125Hz. Does it sound fuller? Does it sound muddy?

I) Cut 2 dB at 125Hz. Does it blend better in the mix? Did it lose its fullness?

E7.2: EQing The Snare - Part 2

Let's try some subtractive EQing. For this exercise, you'll need to solo just the snare drum.

A) Set the *Boost/Cut* control to a moderate level of cut (8 or 10 dB should work.)

B) Sweep through the frequencies until you find the frequency where the sound has the least amount of boxiness and the most definition.

C) Adjust the amount of cut to taste.

D) Set the *Boost/Cut* control to a moderate level of boost (8 or 10 dB should work.)

E) Sweep through the frequencies until you find the frequency where the sound jumps out. Stay on this frequency.

F) Decrease the boost to 0 db, then cut 2 dB at that frequency. Does the sound seem more natural? Does the sound seem to have more low end? Does it seem to have more high end?

G) Now cut 4 dB at that frequency. Does the sound seem more natural? Does the sound seem to have more low end? Does it seem to have more high end?

H) Now cut 6 dB at that frequency. Does the sound seem more natural? Does the sound seem to have more low end? Does it seem to have more high end? Does it now seem to be missing something?

I) Un-solo the snare. How does it sound in the mix? Does it blend better? Does it sound more or less natural? Is it masked by other drums or cymbals?

E7.3: EQing The Kick

Once again, solo the entire drum kit either individually or via the group or subgroup.

A) Can you hear the kick distinctly? Is it crisp and full sounding, or flabby and hollow?

B) Cut 2 dB at 400Hz. Does it blend better in the mix? Does it sound less hollow? Is it more defined?

C) Cut 4 dB at 400Hz. Does it blend better in the mix? Does it sound less hollow? Is it more defined?

D) Sweep the frequencies between 200 and 600Hz. Is there a frequency that works better than 400Hz?

E) Cut 6 dB at the frequency you found. Does it blend better in the mix? Does it sound less hollow? Is it more defined? Did it lose some fullness?

F) Add 2 dB at 60Hz. Does it sound fuller or boomy?

G) Cut 2 dB at 60Hz. Does it sound more distinct or is it lacking bottom end?

H) Add 4 dB at 60Hz. Does it sound fuller or boomy?

I) Cut 5 dB at 60Hz. Does it sound more distinct or is it lacking bottom end?

J) Try cutting and boosting by 2, 4 and 6 dB at 80, 100 and 120Hz. Can the kick be heard better in the mix? Does it sound full or thin?

K) Add 2 dB at 5kHz. Does it come forward in the mix? Does it sound tinny or too bright?

L) Sweep the frequencies between 1k and 10kHz. At what point is it most distinct sounding?

M) Insert the low-pass filter and set it for 40Hz. Does the kick sound more distinct? Did it lose its bottom?

N) Insert the low pass filter and set it for 60Hz. Does the kick sound more distinct? Did it lose its bottom? Does it sound better in the mix? Does the mix sound better?

E7.4: EQing The Rack Toms

Once again, solo the entire drum kit either individually or via the group or subgroup.

A) Can you hear each rack tom distinctly? Is it crisp and full sounding, or flabby and hollow?

B) Proceed as in exercise E7.3 in +/- 2 dB increments at 500Hz and 5kHz. Sweep the frequencies around each to find the best spot.

C) Insert the low-pass filter and set it for 60Hz. Does the tom sound more distinct? Did it lose its bottom?

D) Insert the low-pass filter and set it for 100Hz. Does the tom sound more distinct? Did it lose its bottom? Do they fit better in the mix? Does the mix sound better?

E7.5: EQing The Floor Tom

Once again, solo the entire drum kit either individually or via the group or subgroup.

A) Can you hear each floor tom distinctly? Is it crisp and full sounding, or flabby and hollow?

B) Proceed as in Exercise E7.3 in +/- 2 dB increments at 80Hz and 5kHz. Sweep the frequencies around each to find the best spot.

C) Insert the low-pass filter and set it for 40Hz. Does the floor tom sound more distinct? Did it lose its bottom?

D) Insert the low-pass filter and set it for 60Hz. Does the floor tom sound more distinct? Did it lose its bottom? Does it fit better in the mix? Does the mix sound better?

E7.6: EQing The Hi-Hat

Once again, solo the entire drum kit either individually or via the group or subgroup.

A) Can you hear the hi-hat distinctly? Is it crisp and full sounding, or flabby and hollow?

B) Proceed as in exercise E7.3 in +/- 2 dB increments at 200Hz and 10kHz. Sweep the frequencies around each to find the best spot. Does it sound fuller, or does it clang?

C) Insert the low-pass filter and set it for 60Hz. Does the hi-hat sound more distinct? Did it lose its bottom?

D) Insert the low-pass filter and set it for 120Hz. Does the hi-hat sound more distinct? Did it lose its bottom? Does it fit better in the mix? Does the mix sound better?

E7.7: EQing The Cymbal Or Overhead Mics

Once again, solo the entire drum kit either individually or via the group or subgroup.

A) Can you hear the cymbals distinctly? Are they crisp and full sounding, or flabby and hollow?

B) Proceed as in exercise E7.3 in +/- 2 dB increments at 200Hz and 10kHz. Sweep the frequencies around each to find the best spot. Do they sound fuller, or do they clang?

C) Insert the low-pass filter and set it for 60Hz. Do the cymbals sound more distinct? Did they lose their low end? Do they sound better?

D) Insert the low-pass filter and set it for 120Hz. Do the cymbals sound more distinct? Did they lose their low end? Do they sound better? Do they fit better in the mix? Does the mix sound better?

Equalizing The Bass

The bass provides the power to the mix, but it's the relationship between it and drums that really makes a mix sound big and fat. That's why some mixers will spend hours just trying to fine tune this balance, because if the relationship isn't correct, then the song will just never sound big and punchy.

At its simplest, EQing the bass at a higher frequency (like 100Hz) and the kick at a lower one (like 60 or 80Hz) or vice-verse can work, however it's usually a matter of using the frequency juggling method of EQing to find the frequencies that work the best.

The most common frequencies for bass guitar are anywhere from 50 to 100Hz for bottom, attack at 700Hz, and finger snap at 2.5kHz.

Exercise Pod - EQing The Bass

E7.8: A) Solo the bass and drums and raise the monitor level so it's a little louder than what you'd usually listen at. Can you hear the bass well? Does it mask the kick? Can you hear each note distinctly?

B) Solo the kick and the bass. Can you hear the bass well? Does it mask the kick? Can you hear each note distinctly? Does the bass mask the kick?

C) Wherever you cut a frequency on the kick, boost that frequency on the bass. In other words, if you cut at 400Hz, boost the bass by 2 dB increments in this spot. Can you hear the bass and kick distinctly? Do they reinforce one another?

D) If the kick is boosted at 80Hz, boost the bass at 100 or 120Hz. Can you hear the bass and kick distinctly? Do they reinforce one another?

E) What happens if you switch these frequencies? In other words, if you boost the kick at 100 and the bass at 80Hz. Can you hear the bass and kick distinctly? Do they reinforce one another?

F) Does it sound fuller if you add 2 dB at 60Hz? Does it sound muddy? Does it mask the kick?

G) Insert the high pass filter and set it to 60Hz. Is the bass more distinct? What happens if you move the frequency to 80Hz?

H) Does the bass fit better with the kick if you boost it around 700Hz? Does it fit better if you add 2 dB at around 2.5kHz? Is it more distinct sounding?

I) Add the rest of the drum kit. Can you hear the bass distinctly? Does it mask any other drum? Does it reinforce the kick drum? If so, check where the offending drum is EQed. Cut the frequency on the bass wherever it's boosted on the clashing drum and boost wherever it's cut.

J) If the bass still isn't heard distinctly, make sure that it's not boosted at the same frequency as any of the drums.

Equalizing The Vocal

The vocal is almost always the focal point of the song, so not only is it important that it's heard well in the mix, but it has to sound good as well. That being said, what works on a male vocal won't necessarily work on a female.

EQing can make a vocalist sound up close and in your face, or back in the mix, so it depends up the song and the arrangement before you choose the frequencies that best work for the song.

A small boost at 125 to 250Hz can make the voice sound a bit more "chesty." Boosting between 2kHz to 5kHz accentuates the consonants and adds presence, which makes the vocal seem closer to the listener. The frequencies that cause sibilance are anywhere from 4kHz to 7kHz, and what's known as "air" is between 10k to 15kHz.

As for background vocals, cutting a few dB at 2kHz to 5kHz can separate them from the lead vocal, if that's what the song requires.

Exercise Pod - EQing The Vocal

E7.9: Listen to the vocal against the entire mix. Is the sound of the vocal too thick or too thin?

A) If the vocal seems too big or thick, cut a few dB at around 125Hz for a male, and around 250Hz for a female. Does it fit better in the mix now? Does it sound thin?

B) If the vocal needs to be thicker or bigger sounding, add a few dB at those frequencies. Does it fit better in the mix now? Does it sound too thick?

C) If the "P"s, "F"s and "S"s are distinct, add a dB or two between 4k and 7kHz. Does it fit better in the mix now? Does it sound strident or sibilant?

D) If the "S"s are too bright, try cutting a dB or two between 4k and 7kHz. More than that and the vocal will lose intelligibility. Use a de-esser instead.

E) To brighten the vocal, add 2 dB at 10kHz. What does it sound like? If you can't hear it do anything, then add a little more.

F) Add 2 dB at 12kHz instead. What does it sound like? Does it fit better in the mix now? Does it sound tinny?

G) Add 2 dB at 15kHz instead. What does it sound like? Can you hear it at all?

H) Insert a HPF at 60Hz. Is the vocal cleaner? Is the mix cleaner? Does the vocal sound different? Does it lack bottom?

I) Insert a HPF at 100Hz. Is the vocal cleaner? Is the mixer cleaner? Does the vocal sound different? Does it lack bottom?

E7.10: Listen to the vocal against the entire mix. Is there another instrument clashing against it frequency-wise? If so, solo the vocal and the instrument that's clashing with it.

A) Look at the EQ of both tracks. Is there a boost at the same spot? If so, decrease the boost or even cut at that frequency. Can you hear both tracks more distinctly? Can you hear the vocal better? Does it fit better in the mix now? Does it sound thin?

B) Alternately, look at the EQ of both tracks. Is there a boost at the same spot? If so, adjust the frequency of the track conflicting with the vocal either up or down a little. Can you hear both tracks more distinctly? Can you hear the vocal better?

C) Is the EQ cut on the vocal track the same as where it's boosted on the offending track? If so, move the frequency of the offending track up or down a little. Can you hear both tracks more distinctly? Can you hear the vocal better?

E7.11: If there are no frequency boosts or cuts that are conflicting, but a conflict still exists, listen closely to both channels. Is the conflict in the high or low frequencies?

A) If the conflict is in the lower frequencies, insert a HPF in the signal path of the offending channel and sweep the frequencies from 60 to 200Hz. Is the conflict still there? If not, is the sound of the instrument still acceptable?

B) Alternately, insert a HPF in the signal path of the vocal channel and sweep the frequencies from 60 to 200Hz. Is the conflict still there? If not, is the sound of the vocal still acceptable? What happens if the HPF is inserted on both channels?

C) If the conflict is in the higher frequencies, set a mid-frequency EQ to 6 dB of cut, and sweep the frequencies between 1k and 5kHz. Is there a spot where the conflict goes away? If so, decrease the cut just to the point where you can hear the frequency conflict, then back it off a bit. Can you hear both channels distinctly? Do they both sound acceptable?

D) Un-solo both channels and listen with the rest of the track. Can you hear both tracks distinctly? Is there any other conflicts? If so, solo the tracks that are conflicting and repeat steps A through D.

E7.12: Listen to the vocal against the entire mix. Does the vocal seem forward enough in the mix?

A) Add 2 dB at between 2k and 5kHz. Does it seem to come forward in the mix?

B) What happens if you add more than 2 dB? Does it fit better in the mix now? Does it sound thin?

Exercise Pod - EQing the Background Vocals

E7.13: If the background vocals are conflicting with the lead vocal, solo all vocal and background vocal channels.

A) On the background vocal tracks, set a mid-frequency EQ to 6 dB of cut, and sweep the frequencies between 2k and 5kHz. Is there a spot where the conflict goes away? If so, decrease the cut just to the point where you can hear the frequency conflict, then back it off a bit. Can you hear both channels distinctly? Do they both sound acceptable?

B) If the conflict is in the lower frequencies, insert a HPF in the signal path of the offending channel and sweep the frequencies from 60 to 200Hz. Is the conflict still there? If not, is the sound of the instrument still acceptable?

Equalizing The Electric Guitar

Electric guitars, whether they are clean or distorted, are very dependent upon how they sit in the track with other instruments in order to be heard in the mix. In some cases, like when a distorted guitar is playing power chords, it may be better for the guitar to blend in with the rest of the instruments rather than be heard distinctly, while at other times you want to be sure to hear every note.

Frequencies to check out are around 240 to 500Hz, which provides fullness, and 1.5kHz to 2.5kHz which gives it presence. Guitar amplifiers that are miked rarely have much useful information below 150Hz or above about 8kHz, so it's best to filter out above and below those frequencies.

Exercise Pod - EQing The Electric Guitar

E7.14: Listen to the guitar against the entire mix. Is there another instrument clashing against it frequency-wise? If so, solo the guitar and the instrument that's clashing with it.

A) Look at the EQ of both tracks. Is there a boost at the same spot? If so, decrease the boost or even cut at that frequency. Can you hear both tracks more distinctly? Can you hear the vocal better?

B) Alternately, look at the EQ of both tracks. Is there a boost at the same spot? If so, adjust the frequency of the track conflicting with the vocal either up or down a little. Can you hear both tracks more distinctly? Can you hear the guitar better?

C) Is the EQ cut on the vocal track where it's boosted on the offending track? If so, move the frequency up or down a little. Can you hear both tracks more distinctly? Can you hear the guitar better?

E7.15: If there are no boosts or cuts that are conflicting, but the frequency conflict still exists, listen closely to both channels. Is the conflict in the high or low frequencies?

A) If the conflict is in the lower frequencies, insert a HPF in the signal path of the offending channel and sweep the frequencies from 60 to 200Hz. Is the conflict still there? If not, is the sound of the instrument still acceptable?

B) Alternately, insert a HPF in the signal path of the guitar channel and sweep the frequencies from 60 to 200Hz. Is the conflict still there? If not, is the sound of the guitar still acceptable? What happens if the HPF is inserted on both channels?

C) If the conflict remains in the lower frequencies, set a mid-frequency EQ to 6 dB of cut, and sweep the frequencies between 100Hz and 1kHz. Is there a spot where the conflict goes away? If so, decrease the cut just to the point where you can hear the frequency conflict, then back it off a bit. Can you hear both channels distinctly? Do they both sound acceptable?

D) If the conflict is in the higher frequencies, set a mid-frequency EQ to 6 dB of cut, and sweep the frequencies between 1 and 5kHz. Is there a spot where the conflict goes away? If so, decrease the cut just to the point where you can hear the frequency conflict, then back it off a bit. Can you hear both channels distinctly? Do they both sound acceptable?

D) Un-solo both channels and listen with the rest of the track. Can you hear both tracks distinctly? Is there any other conflicts? If so, solo the tracks that are conflicting and repeat steps A through D.

Equalizing The Acoustic Guitar

The acoustic guitar has an entirely different sound from an electric guitar and therefore has to be approached differently. Plus, each acoustic guitar has its own sound depending upon the body size and wood that it's made from.

For instance, the bigger the guitar body (like a dreadnought or jumbo size), the more bottom end it will have, which might sound great live but could muddy up a recording. On the other hand, a small body or cutaway acoustic guitar will have less bass but may sit better in a track as a result. The same goes for the wood that it's made from. A guitar made from rosewood will have much more body, while one made of mahogany may sound thinner, yet record better.

Like other instruments, there are certain frequencies to look at when EQing an acoustic. At 80Hz you'll get fullness, while you'll hear more of the body at 240Hz. The presence of the instrument can be found between 2kHz to 5kHz, 5 to 8kHz will make it cut through a mix, while 10kHz will accentuate any finger noises.

Exercise Pod - EQing The Acoustic Guitar

E7.16: Listen to the guitar against the entire mix. Is there another instrument clashing against it frequency-wise? If so, solo the guitar and the instrument that's clashing with it.

A) Look at the EQ of both tracks. Is there a boost at the same spot? If so, decrease the boost or even cut at that frequency. Can you hear both tracks more distinctly? Can you hear the guitar better in the mix?

B) Alternately, look at the EQ of both tracks. Is there a boost at the same spot? If so, adjust the frequency of the track conflicting with the vocal either up or down a little. Can you hear both tracks more distinctly? Can you hear the acoustic guitar better in the mix?

C) Is the EQ cut on the vocal track where it's boosted on the offending track? If so, move the frequency up or down a little. Can you hear both tracks more distinctly? Can you hear the acoustic guitar better in the mix?

E7.17: If there's no boost or cuts that are conflicting yet a frequency conflict still exists, listen closely to both channels. Is the conflict in the high or low frequencies?

A) If the conflict is in the lower frequencies, insert a HPF in the signal path of the offending channel and sweep the frequencies from 60 to 200Hz. Is the conflict still there? If not, is the sound of the instrument still acceptable?

B) Alternately, insert a HPF in the signal path of the guitar channel and sweep the frequencies from 60 to 100Hz. Is the conflict still there? If not, is the sound of the guitar still acceptable? What happens if the HPF is inserted on both channels?

C) If the conflict remains in the lower frequencies, set a mid-frequency EQ to 6 dB of cut, and sweep the frequencies between 60Hz and 1KHz. Is there a spot where the conflict goes away? If so, decrease the cut just to the point where you can hear the frequency conflict, then back it off a bit. Can you hear both instruments distinctly? Do they both sound acceptable?

D) If the conflict is in the higher frequencies, set a mid-frequency EQ to 6 dB of cut, and sweep the frequencies between 1kHz and 8kHz. Is there a spot where the conflict goes away? If so, decrease the cut just to the point where you can hear the frequency conflict, then back it off a bit. Can you hear both channels distinctly? Do they both sound acceptable?

D) Unsolo both channels and listen with the rest of the track. Can you hear both tracks distinctly? Are there any other conflicts? If so, solo the tracks that are conflicting and repeat steps A through D.

Equalizing The Piano

The grand piano is an interesting instrument because it's so percussive and has such a wide frequency range. It can also play just about any role in an arrangement, from blending into the rhythm section, to being the pad element when played with long sustained chords or notes, to being the lead or fill element. This versatility, combined with the differing sounds you can get from a piano through various miking methods, opens it up to a variety of EQ treatments, depending on the situation. (see Figure 7.3). That said, the piano generally sounds full at around 80Hz and has presence at 3kHz to 5kHz, although too much boost in this frequency can give it a honky-tonk quality.

Figure 7.3: Typical Piano Miking

Exercise Pod - EQing The Piano

E7.18: Follow the method outlined in E7.16 and E7.17, being especially aware of the 80 to 100Hz and 2kHz to 5kHz regions.

Equalizing The Organ

As stated in Chapter 4, the organ is a quintessential instrument for the pad element of an arrangement. As a result, it's usually used as sort of a "glue" in the track and isn't always heard as a distinct instrument. It does have a wide frequency range though, and can have a huge low end, so care must be taken so it doesn't get in the way of the bass guitar or kick drum (see Figure 7.4). You'll hear fullness at 80Hz, body at 240Hz, and presence at 2kHz to 5kHz. It's not uncommon to use a HPF to roll off the low end below 100Hz.

Exercise Pod - EQing The Organ

E7.19: Follow the method outlined in E7.16 and E7.17, being especially aware of the 80 to 100Hz and 2kHz to 5kHz regions.

Equalizing Strings

Whether real or artificial, strings are frequently used as the finishing touch to an arrangement and frequently used as the pad element, although they tend to stick out of a mix more than an organ because of their mostly high-frequency content. Fullness comes at around 250Hz, they tend to get shrill at around 5kHz and scratchy sounding between 7kHz and 10kHz. Sometimes a little cut at 4kHz to 5kHz eliminates any harshness. Unless the section includes basses, a high-pass filter can work wonders for cleaning up the sound.

Figure 7.4: A Hammond A100 With A Leslie Speaker, Which Gives The Organ It's Big Low End

Exercise Pod - EQing The String Section

E7.20: Follow the method outlined in E7.16 and E7.17, being especially aware of the 200 to 250Hz, 4kHz to 5kHz, and 7kHz to 10kHz regions.

Equalizing Horns

Both brass and woodwinds contain mostly mid-range frequency content, so they can easily conflict with guitars, vocals and snare drums. While fullness comes at 120Hz, they can sound very piercing at 5kHz (especially for brass instruments). Once again, an HPF can greatly clean up the sound.

Exercise Pod - EQing Horns

E7.21: Follow the method outlined in E7.16 and E7.17, being especially aware of the 100 to 150Hz and 3kHz to 6kHz regions.

Equalizing Percussion

Percussion can be categorized into two groups, the low-frequency drum instruments like bongos, congas, djembe (see Figure 7.5) and udu; and high-frequency instruments like shakers, tambourines and triangles. While each of these instruments have different frequency points, they can also easily conflict with other instruments in the mix.

Percussion instruments can easily compete for frequency space with the drum kit, guitars, vocals and strings. Although they're very important to a mix because of the musical motion they convey, care must be taken when EQing them.

Generally speaking, the ring that bongos and congas sometimes have can be accentuated at 200Hz, while the slap comes at 5kHz. For for high frequency percussion like shakers, 5kHz to 8kHz usually will make them more present. There's not normally much energy below 500Hz to 1kHz, so using the HPF below this point won't affect the sound at all while cleaning up some unwanted artifacts captured during recording.

Figure 7.5: A Djembe Drum

Exercise Pod - EQing Bongos And Congas

E7.22: Follow the method outlined in E7.16 and E7.17, being especially aware of the 150 to 250Hz and 5kHz to 8kHz regions.

Exercise Pod - EQing Shakers And Triangle

E7.23: Follow the method outlined in E7.16 and E7.17, being especially aware of using a HPF from 100Hz to 1kHz and EQing at 5kHz to 10kHz regions.

CHAPTER 8
ADDING REVERB

Like with other aspects of mixing, the use of reverb is frequently either overlooked or misunderstood. Reverb is added to a track to create width and depth, but also to dress up an otherwise boring sound. The real secret is how much to use and how to adjust its various parameters.

Reverb Basics

Before we get into adding and adjusting the reverb in your mix, let's look at some of the reasons to add reverb first.

When you get right down to it, there are four reasons to add reverb.

1. To make the recorded track sound like it's in a specific acoustic environment. Many times a track is recorded in an acoustic space that doesn't fit the song or the final vision of the mixer. You may record in a small dead room but want it to sound like it was in a large studio, a small and reflective drum room, or a live and reflective church. Reverb will take you to each of those environments and many more.

2. To add some personality and excitement to a recorded sound. Picture reverb as makeup on a model. She may look rather plain or even only mildly attractive until the makeup makes her gorgeous by covering her blemishes, highlighting her eyes, and accentuating her lips and cheekbones. Reverb does the same thing with some tracks. It can make the blemishes less noticeable, change the texture of the sound itself, and highlight it in a new way.

3. To make a track sound bigger or wider than it really is. Anything that's recorded in stereo automatically sounds bigger and wider than something recorded in mono, because the natural ambience of the recording environment is captured. In order to keep the track count and data-storage requirements down, most instrument or vocal recordings are done in mono. As a result, the space has to be added artificially by reverb. Usually, reverb that has a short decay time (less than one second) will make a track sound bigger.

4. To move a track further back in the mix. While panning takes you from left to right in the stereo spectrum, reverb will take you from front to rear (see Figure 8.1). An easy way to understand how this works is to picture a band on stage. If you want the singer to sound like he's in front of the drum kit, you would add some reverb to the kit. If you wanted the horn section to sound like it was placed behind the kit, you'd add more reverb. If you wanted the singer to sound like he's in between the drums and the horns, you'd leave the drums dry and add a touch of reverb to the vocal, but less than the horns.

If we were going to get more sophisticated with this kind of layering, we'd use different reverbs for each of the instruments and tailor the parameters to best fit the sound we're going after.

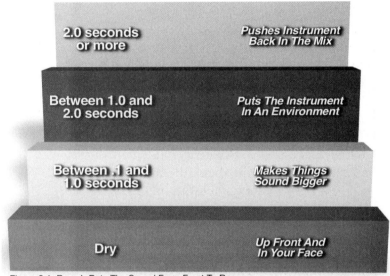

Figure 8.1: Reverb Puts The Sound From Front To Rear

Typical Reverb Parameters

One of the mistakes that many beginning mixers make is to simply add the reverb and never attempt to adjust it to make it work better with the track. While some sophisticated reverbs have exotic parameters like *Spin* and *Dampening* that can confuse all but the select few engineers, if you concentrate on just a few of the parameters that make the biggest difference in the sound, and that are commonly found on most reverbs, you'll find that adjusting it gets a lot easier (see Figure 8.2).

The Major Parameter Controls

Although many sophisticated reverbs have a wide variety of somewhat obscure parameters, you can get exactly what you need for any mix with only the following five:

Reverb Type: Most variable software reverbs have four environments that you can dial in; hall, room, chamber and plate. A hall is a large space that has a long decay time and lots of reflections to it. A room is a much smaller space that can be dead or reflective, but it has a short decay time of about 1.5 seconds or less. An acoustic chamber is an electronic representation of a tiled room that many of the large studios used to specially build to create a great reverb sound (see Figure 8.3). Phil Spector's "Wall of Sound" was built around an excellent acoustic chamber at Gold Star Studios, for example. A plate is a 4-foot hanging piece of metal with transducers on it that many studios used for artificial reverb when they couldn't afford to build a chamber (see Figure 8.4).

Each of these reverb types have a distinctly different sound and there's no rule on which one to use. In most reverb plug-ins available today, you can usually just find one that you like and adjust the parameters to fit almost any song, or you can be more adventurous and try a different setting for every song. Either works.

Decay Time: The decay time represents how long it takes the reverb tail to fall off to where we can no longer hear it. Longer delay times push a track further back in the mix, while short ones (under about one second) make it sound bigger.

Pre-Delay: This parameter delays the entrance of the reverb. A Pre-delay not only makes the reverb sound larger, but it keeps the reverb from clouding up the mix by allowing the listener to hear the attack of the sound clearly before the reverb kicks in. In the days before electronic reverbs, pre-delay was achieved by sending a signal to a tape recorder then setting the delay by altering the playback speed. Pre-delay can be usually be adjusted from 0 to about 120 milliseconds or so, which is about an eighth of a second.

High- and Low-Pass Filters: Though often overlooked, the high- and low-pass filters are the parameters that let you shape the tone of the reverb so that it fits better in the mix. If you want to clearly hear the reverb, you typically wouldn't roll off the high-end much so it can stick out of the mix a bit. On the other hand, if you wanted the reverb to blend in better, you'd use the LPF to roll-off the highs anywhere from 10k to as low as 2kHz.

On the other hand, if your mix has a lot of low end and is already busy, too much low end on the reverb would just muddy it up. That's why you'd use the HPF to roll it off anywhere from 50Hz to as high as 600Hz. As an example, the famous Abbey Road Studios reverbs that have been heard on hundreds of hit records over the last 50 plus years (including every Beatles record), set their LPF at 10kHz and their HPF at 600Hz.

If a reverb that you're using doesn't have its own built-in filters, you can always insert an equalizer or filter into the send or the return channel and roll the frequencies off there, or even boost them if needed.

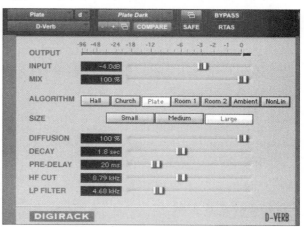

Figure 8.2: Typical Reverb Parameter Controls

Figure 8.3: An Example Of An Acoustic Chamber

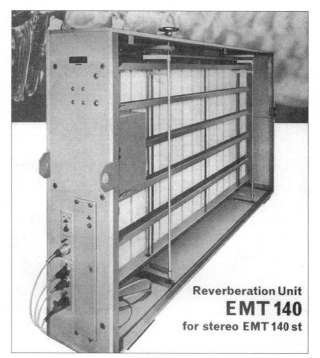

Figure 8.4: An EMT 140 Plate Reverb

Dry/Wet: The *dry/wet* control (sometimes called *mix*) allows you to mix the reverb signal with the dry signal. This is essential for dialing in the correct amount of reverb if the plug-in is inserted on a track, but it's normally set to 100 percent wet when inserted into a dedicated effects return channel.

Many reverbs also include a parameter known as *diffusion*, which simulates how reflective the walls in a particular space are. For instance, a more diffuse environment has hard walls with a lot of reflections, while one with softer walls has fewer reflections. A simple way to think of it is that high diffusion provides a thicker sounding reverb, and low diffusion is thinner sounding.

Timing A Reverb To The Track

One of the secrets of hit-making engineers is that they time the reverb to the track. That means timing both the pre-delay and the decay so it "breathes" with the pulse of the track. Here's how it's done.

Timing The Decay

The decay of a reverb is timed to the track by triggering it off of a snare hit and adjusting the decay parameter so that the decay just dies by the next snare hit. The idea is to make the decay breathe with the track.

Exercise Pod - Timing Reverb Decay

Before you begin any of the exercises in this chapter, be sure to have two reverbs with the sends and returns already set up. Set one reverb to "Room" (we'll call it Reverb #1) and the other to "Hall" (Reverb #2). Refer to your DAW or console manual on how to do this.

E8.1: Solo the snare drum and the reverb returns (or put them into *Solo Safe* - refer to your DAW or console manual on how to do this). Be sure that the *Dry/Wet* control is set to 100% wet, and the return levels are set at about -10.

A) Raise the level of the send to the Room reverb until the reverb can be clearly heard. Does the snare sound distant? Does it sound bigger than before?

B) Adjust the *Decay* parameter until the reverb dies out before the next snare hit of the song. Does the snare sound clearer?

C) Mute the send to the Room reverb and raise the level to the Hall reverb. Does the snare sound distant? Does it sound bigger than before? Does it sound bigger than the Room reverb?

D) Adjust the *Decay* parameter until the reverb dies out before the next snare hit of the song. Does the snare sound clearer? Does it sound bigger?

E) Adjust the *Decay* parameter until the reverb dies out before the 2nd next snare hit after the initial hit. Does the snare sound clearer? Does it sound bigger?

Timing The Pre-delay

Timing the pre-delay to the beat of the track can add depth without the reverb being noticeable. You can time the pre-delay to the track by using the following formula:

7,500/the beats per minute of the track = delay time in milliseconds

As an example:

7,500/125 BPM = 60 milliseconds

This is the delay of a 32nd note. If that's too long, you can divide the result of the formula (60 milliseconds) by 2 to get a 64th note delay of 30 milliseconds. Or double it for a delay of a 16th note at 120 milliseconds. Any other amount that's divisible, like 45 ms or 90 ms, will also sound pretty good.

Another way to time the pre-delay to the track is to use the Ultimate Delay Time iPhone application.

Exercise Pod - Timing Reverb Pre-Delay

E8.2: Solo the snare drum and the reverb returns (or put them into *Solo Safe* —refer to your DAW or console manual on how to do this). Be sure that the *Dry/Wet* control is set to 100% wet, and the return levels are set at about -10.

A) Find the BPM of the song by using the tap feature found on most DAWs or the tap function of a smartphone app like Ultimate Delay Time.

B) Use the formula found above (7,500/song BPM) to find the pre-delay time.

C) Adjust the *Pre-delay* parameter of the Room reverb. Does the snare sound bigger? Does it sound more distinct? Can you hear the attack better?

D) Un-solo the snare and the reverb returns. Does the snare sound bigger when mixed in the track? Does it sound more distinct? Can you hear the attack better?

E) Divide the reverb time by 2 and adjust the *Pre-delay* parameter to this number (for example, 20 ms). Does the snare sound bigger in the track? Does it sound more distinct? Can you hear the attack better?

F) Take your original pre-delay time and multiply it by 2 (for example, 80 ms). Does the snare sound bigger in the track? Does it sound more distinct? Can you hear the attack better?

Figure 8.5:
The Two Reverb Setup

Reverb Setup

As we spoke about in Chapter 2, setting up your reverbs before you begin to mix can be a huge time saver. You'll have to make a few final tweaks as you go along, but that happens with just about every parameter of a mix anyway. Here are a couple of methods.

The Two-Reverb Quick-Setup Method

This setup is designed to get you up and running quickly, with the parameters in a general position to where they almost always sound at least acceptable, and sometimes even surprisingly good (see Figure 8.5). This method works well when you're tracking and need some quick reverb, or for doing rough mixes when you don't have time for a more complete setup. It uses two different reverbs.

Reverb One: This reverb will be used just for the drums. Set it to a "Room" with the decay at 1.5 seconds and a pre-delay of 20 milliseconds. If a HPF is available, set it to 10kHz or even 8kHz. If a LPF is available, set it to 100Hz.

Reverb Two: This reverb is meant for all other instruments and vocals. Set it to a "Plate" with a 1.8 second decay time and a pre-delay of 20 milliseconds. If a HPF is available, set it to 10kHz or even 8kHz. If a LPF is available, set it to 100Hz.

It's surprising how good everything can sound with this quick setup.

The Three-Reverb Full-Setup Method

Many mixers like to have a lot of reverb options available when they mix, so they'll sometimes have three hardware units or plug-ins set to go, which they tweak as they go along (See Figure 8.6). Here's the general setup.

Reverb One: Set it to a "Room" with the decay set at .5 seconds and a pre-delay of around 20 milliseconds. If a HPF is available, set it to 10kHz or even 8kHz. If a LPF is available, set it to 100Hz, but adjust as needed for the track.

Reverb Two: Set it to a "Plate" with around a 1.5 second decay time and a pre-delay that's timed to the track. If a HPF is available, set it to 10kHz or even 8kHz. If a LPF is available, set it to 100Hz, but adjust as needed for the track.

Reverb Three: Set it to a "Hall" with around a 2.2 second decay time and a pre-delay that's timed to the track. If a HPF is available, set it to 10kHz or even 8kHz. If a LPF is available, set it to 100Hz, but adjust as needed for the track.

This is a starting place for these reverb settings as they will be tweaked for the track as the mix progresses. Also, these reverbs are not intended for any particular instrument. Since many mixes end up using several reverbs that are set to short, medium and long decays, this setup just puts the plug-ins in the ballpark waiting for you to decide how to use them later.

Adding Reverb To Instruments

There's no rule for where and how reverb is added to a mix. In some mixes, a single reverb can work for every instrument and vocal (just like in all those great hits of 1950s, '60s and '70s), while another mix might sound better with a separate reverb for every mix element. Let's try a few exercises that will use each scenario.

Figure 8.6: The Three Reverb Setup

Adding Reverb To The Drum Kit

The drum kit is interesting and different from the other instruments in the mix in that it may use several different reverbs in order for it to lay correctly in the track. For instance, the kick drum may be left completely dry, while the snare drum may have its own separate reverb, or an additional one from what the rest of the kit uses. In fact, the cymbals and hat may also have more of a room sound, while the toms may be larger and put further back in the mix.

Then on the other hand, a single reverb may be just enough to make the kit sound great.

Exercise Pod - Adding Reverb To The Drum Kit

Solo the entire drum kit and the reverb returns (or put them into solo safe - refer to your DAW or console manual on how to do this). Be sure that the dry/wet control is set to 100% wet, and the return levels are set at about -10.

E8.3: Adding Reverb To The Snare Drum.

A) What kind of sound are you looking for? Do you want the snare to sound bigger or do you want to push it back in the mix?

B) Raise the level of the send to the Room reverb until the reverb can be clearly heard. Does it sound distant? Does it sound bigger than before? Does it seem to move behind the other instruments? Does it sound better with no reverb at all? Does it fit better in the track when you un-solo the drums so you can hear them with the track?

C) Does it sound better when sent to the Hall reverb instead? Does it sound distant? Does it sound bigger than before? Does it seem to move behind the other instruments? Does it sound better with no reverb at all? Does it fit better in the track when you un-solo the drums so you can hear them with the track?

D) What does it sound like with both reverbs? Does it sound distant? Does it sound bigger than before? Does it seem to move behind the other instruments? Does it sound better with no reverb at all? Does it fit better in the track when you un-solo the drums so you can hear them with the track?

E) What happens if you lower or raise the *Pre-delay* setting? Does it sound distant? Does it sound bigger than before? Does it seem to move behind the other instruments? Does it sound better with no reverb at all? Does it fit better in the track when you un-solo the drums so you can hear them with the track?

F) What does it sound like if you lower or raise the *Decay* setting? Does it sound distant? Does it sound bigger than before? Does it seem to move behind the other instruments? Does it sound better with no reverb at all? Does it fit better in the track when you un-solo the drums so you can hear them with the track?

G) After choosing the reverb and its settings, listen to the snare with the rest of the mix. Add enough reverb so that you can just hear it if any is needed. You'll dial in the correct amount later, after the reverb is added to the rest of the instruments.

E8.4: Adding Reverb To The Kick Drum.

A) What kind of sound are you looking for? Do you want the kick to sound bigger or do you want to push it back in the mix?

B) Raise the level of the send to the Room reverb until the reverb can be clearly heard. Does the kick sound distant? Does it sound bigger than before? Does it seem to move behind the other instruments? Does it sound better with no reverb at all? Does it fit better in the track when you un-solo the drums so you can hear them with the track?

C) Does the kick sound better when sent to the Hall reverb instead? Does it sound distant? Does it sound bigger than before? Does it seem to move behind the other instruments? Does it sound better with no reverb at all? Does it fit better in the track when you un-solo the drums so you can hear them with the track?

D) What does the kick sound like with both reverbs applied? Does it sound distant? Does it sound bigger than before? Does it seem to move behind the other instruments? Does it sound better with no reverb at all? Does it fit better in the track when you un-solo the drums so you can hear them with the track?

E) What happens if you lower or raise the *Pre-delay* setting? Does the kick sound distant? Does it sound bigger than before? Does it seem to move behind the other instruments? Does it sound better with no reverb at all? Does it fit better in the track when you un-solo the drums so you can hear them with the track?

F) What does it sound like if you lower or raise the *Decay* setting? Does the kick sound distant? Does it sound bigger than before? Does it seem to move behind the other instruments? Does it sound better with no reverb at all? Does it fit better in the track when you un-solo the drums so you can hear them with the track?

G) After choosing the reverb and its settings, listen to the kick with the rest of the mix. Add enough reverb so that you can just hear it if any is needed. You'll dial in the correct amount later after the reverb is added to the rest of the instruments.

E8.5: Adding Reverb To The Toms.

A) What kind of sound are you looking for? Do you want the toms to sound bigger or do you want to push them back in the mix?

B) Raise the level of the send to the Room reverb until the reverb can be clearly heard. Do the toms sound distant? Do they sound bigger than before? Do they seem to move behind the other instruments? Do they sound better with no reverb at all? Do they fit better in the track when you un-solo the drums so you can hear them with the track?

C) Do the toms sound better when sent to the Hall reverb instead? Do they sound distant? Do they sound bigger than before? Do they seem to move behind the other instruments? Do they sound better with no reverb at all? Do they fit better in the track when you un-solo the drums so you can hear them with the track?

D) What do the toms sound like with both reverbs? Do they it sound distant? Do they sound bigger than before? Do they seem to move behind the other instruments? Do they sound better with no reverb at all? Do they fit better in the track when you un-solo the drums so you can hear them with the track?

E) What happens if you lower or raise the *Pre-delay* setting? Do the toms sound distant? Do they sound bigger than before? Do they seem to move behind the other instruments? Do they sound better with no reverb at all? Do they fit better in the track when you un-solo the drums so you can hear them with the track?

F) What does it sound like if you lower or raise the *Decay* setting? Do the toms sound distant? Do they sound bigger than before? Do they seem to move behind the other instruments? Do they sound better with no reverb at all? Do they fit better in the track when you un-solo the drums so you can hear them with the track?

G) After choosing the reverb and its settings, listen to the toms with the rest of the mix. Add enough reverb so that you can just hear it if any is needed. You'll dial in the correct amount later after the reverb is added to the rest of the instruments.

E8.6: Adding Reverb To The Cymbals.

A) What kind of sound are you looking for? Do you want the cymbals to sound bigger or do you want to push them back in the mix?

B) Raise the level of the send to the Room reverb until the reverb can be clearly heard. Do the cymbals sound distant? Do they sound bigger than before? Do they seem to move behind the other instruments? Do they sound better with no reverb at all? Do they fit better in the track when you un-solo the drums so you can hear them with the track?

C) Does it sound better when sent to the Hall reverb instead? Do the cymbals sound distant? Do they sound bigger than before? Do they seem to move behind the other instruments? Do they sound better with no reverb at all? Do they fit better in the track when you un-solo the drums so you can hear them with the track?

D) What does it sound like with both reverbs? Do the cymbals sound distant? Do they sound bigger than before? Do they seem to move behind the other instruments? Do they sound better with no reverb at all? Do they fit better in the track when you un-solo the drums so you can hear them with the track?

E) What happens if you lower or raise the *Pre-delay* setting? Do the cymbals sound distant? Do they sound bigger than before? Do they seem to move behind the other instruments? Do they sound better with no reverb at all? Do they fit better in the track when you un-solo the drums so you can hear them with the track?

F) What does it sound like if you lower or raise the *Decay* setting? Do the cymbals sound distant? Do they sound bigger than before? Do they seem to move behind the other instruments? Do they sound better with no reverb at all? Do they fit better in the track when you un-solo the drums so you can hear them with the track?

G) After choosing the reverb and its settings, listen to the cymbals with the rest of the mix. Add enough reverb so that you can just hear it if any is needed. You'll dial in the correct amount later after the reverb is added to the rest of the instruments.

E8.7: Adding Reverb To The Hi-Hat.

A) What kind of sound are you looking for? Do you want the hi-hat to sound bigger or do you want to push it back in the mix?

B) Raise the level of the send to the Room reverb until the reverb can be clearly heard. Does the hi-hat sound distant? Does it sound bigger than before? Does it seem to move behind the other instruments? Does it sound better with no reverb at all? Does it fit better in the track when you un-solo the drums so you can hear them with the track?

C) Does the hi-hat sound better when sent to the Hall reverb instead? Does it sound distant? Does it sound bigger than before? Does it seem to move behind the other instruments? Does it sound better with no reverb at all? Does it fit better in the track when you un-solo the drums so you can hear them with the track?

D) What does the hi-hat sound like with both reverbs? Does it sound distant? Does it sound bigger than before? Does it seem to move behind the other instruments? Does it sound better with no reverb at all? Does it fit better in the track when you un-solo the drums so you can hear them with the track?

E) What happens if you lower or raise the *Pre-delay* setting? Does the high-hat sound distant? Does it sound bigger than before? Does it seem to move behind the other instruments? Does it sound better with no reverb at all? Does it fit better in the track when you un-solo the drums so you can hear them with the track?

F) What does it sound like if you lower or raise the *Decay* setting? Does the high-hat sound distant? Does it sound bigger than before? Does it seem to move behind the other instruments? Does it sound better with no reverb at all? Does it fit better in the track when you un-solo the drums so you can hear them with the track?

G) After choosing the reverb and its settings, listen to the high-hat with the rest of the mix. Add enough reverb so that you can just hear it if any is needed. You'll dial in the correct amount later after the reverb is added to the rest of the instruments.

E8.8: Tweaking The Sound Of The Reverb.

A) What does it sound like if you turn the HPF off? Can you still hear the reverb? Are the drums bigger or smaller sounding? Is the reverb muddy or distinct?

B) What does it sound like if you turn the HPF to 60Hz? Can you still hear the reverb? Are the drums bigger or smaller sounding? Is the reverb muddy or distinct?

C) What does it sound like if you turn the HPF to 100Hz? Can you still hear the reverb? Are the drums bigger or smaller sounding? Is the reverb muddy or distinct?

D) What does it sound like if you turn the HPF to 500Hz? Can you still hear the reverb? Are the drums bigger or smaller sounding? Is the reverb muddy or distinct?

E) What does it sound like if you turn the LPF to 8kHz? Can you still hear the reverb? Are the drums bigger or smaller sounding? Is the reverb muddy or distinct?

F) What does it sound like if you turn the HPF to 4kHz? Can you still hear the reverb? Are the drums bigger or smaller sounding? Is the reverb muddy or distinct?

G) What does it sound like if you turn the HPF to 2kHz? Can you still hear the reverb? Are the drums bigger or smaller sounding? Is the reverb muddy or distinct?

Adding Reverb To The Bass

Since the bass is so important to the power of the song, and because of the abundance of low-frequency information, reverb is rarely added. That doesn't mean there isn't the occasion where it's effective though ("Money," the 1970s hit by the O'Jays, comes to mind). Sometimes a very little bit of a very short room reverb can make the bass sound a bit bigger, or make it sound like the direct bass was recorded with a mic in the same room as the drums. Either way, it's always worth a try to see if a little reverb just might add some magic.

Exercise Pod - Adding Reverb To The Bass

E8.9: Solo the bass and the reverb returns. Make sure the *Decay* and *Pre-delay* are both timed to the track.

A) What kind of sound are you looking for? Do you want the bass to sound bigger or do you want to push it back in the mix?

B) Raise the level of the send to the Room reverb until the reverb can be clearly heard. Does the bass sound distant? Does it sound bigger than before? Does it sound better with no reverb at all? What does it sound like when you un-solo the bass so you can hear it with the track?

C) Mute the Room reverb and raise the send level to the Hall reverb. Does the bass sound better than the Room reverb? Does it sound distant? Does it sound bigger than before?

D) What does the bass sound like with both reverbs added?

E) Raise the Pre-delay setting on the reverb you've chosen. Does the bass sound distant? Does it sound bigger than before? What does it sound like if you lower the Pre-delay setting?

F) What does the bass sound like if you lower or raise the *Decay* setting?

G) Does the bass fit any better in the mix if you raise the HPF?

H) Does it fit any better in the mix if you lower the LPF?

I) After choosing the reverb and it's settings, listen to the bass with the rest of the mix. Add enough reverb so that you can just hear it if any is needed. You'll dial in the correct amount later after the reverb is added to the rest of the instruments.

Adding Reverb To The Vocal

Since the lead vocal is usually the focal point of the song, the reverb setting for it is critical. Pick the right one and it'll add that extra professional-sounding sheen that all hit records have. Pick the wrong one and it'll sound washed out and lost in the track.

Many times a lead vocal has a lot more reverb on it than it seems, but it's disguised by the way its bandwidth is tailored by the HPF and LPF. Other times, it's important to hear the reverb and every effort is made to maintain or even equalize its high-frequency response. Ballads that have a long period of space in between vocal lines will usually benefit from a longer reverb decay that's obvious.

In the end, you're usually trying to put the vocalist in a space and not push her back in the mix, which is the opposite of what you're trying to do with background vocals.

Background vocals sometimes are just put in a space, pushed back in the mix from the lead vocal, or even made bigger than life thanks to a very short (.2 to .4 second) reverb. If the background vocals are singing harmony with the lead vocal, they sometimes need to have the same reverb as the lead vocal, but most of the time you want them to be distinguished separately, so a different reverb is used.

Exercise Pod - Adding Reverb To The Lead Vocal

E8.10: Solo the lead vocal and the reverb returns. Make sure the *Decay* and *Pre-delay* are both timed to the track.

A) What kind of sound are you looking for? Do you want to put the lead vocal in a space, or do you want to push it back in the mix?

B) Raise the level of the send to the Room reverb until the reverb can be clearly heard. Does it put the vocalist in another environment? Does the vocal sound distant? Does it sound better with no reverb at all? What does it sound like when you un-solo the vocal so you can hear it with the track?

C) Mute the Room reverb and raise the send level to the Hall reverb. Does the lead vocal sound better with the Hall than the Room reverb? Does it sound distant? Does the artificial space better fit the track?

D) What does the lead vocal sound like with both reverbs?

E) Raise the Pre-delay setting on the reverb you've chosen. Can you distinguish the vocal better? What does it sound like if you lower the Pre-delay setting? Is the vocal muddy sounding?

F) What does the lead vocal sound like if you lower or raise the Decay setting? Can you hear the vocal more or less clearly?

G) Does the vocal fit any better in the mix if you raise the HPF frequency on the reverb?

H) Does it fit any better in the mix if you lower the LPF frequency on the reverb?

I) After choosing the reverb and it's settings, listen to the lead vocal with the rest of the mix. Add enough reverb so that you can just hear it if any is needed. You'll dial in the correct amount later after the reverb is added to the rest of the instruments.

Exercise Pod - Adding Reverb To The Background Vocals

E8.11: Solo the background vocals and the reverb returns. Make sure the *Decay* and *Pre-delay* are both timed to the track.

A) What kind of sound are you looking for? Do you want to put the background vocals in a space, make them bigger, or push them back in the mix?

B) Raise the level of the send to the Room reverb until the reverb can be clearly heard. Does it put the background vocals in another environment? Do the background vocals vocal sound distant? Does it sound bigger than before? Does it sound better with no reverb at all? Does it sound like the background vocals are behind the lead vocalist? What does it sound like when you play un-solo the vocal so you can hear it with the track?

C) Mute the Room reverb and raise the send level to the Hall reverb. Does it sound better than the Room reverb for the background vocals? Does it make them sound like they're behind the vocalist? Do they sound too distant?

D) What do the background vocals sound like with both reverbs?

E) Raise the *Pre-delay* setting on the reverb you've chosen. Can you distinguish between the lead and background vocal better? What does it sound like if you lower the *Pre-delay* setting? Does it make the vocal sound muddy?

F) What does it sound like if you lower or raise the *Decay* setting? Can you hear the background vocal more or less clearly?

G) Does the background vocal fit any better in the mix if you raise the HPF frequency on the reverb?

H) Does it fit any better in the mix if you lower the LPF frequency on the reverb?

I) After choosing the reverb and its settings, listen to the lead vocal with the rest of the mix. Add enough reverb so that you can just hear it if any is needed. You'll dial in the correct amount later after the reverb is added to the rest of the instruments.

Adding Reverb To Guitars

While guitars are percussive by nature, they also can have a sustaining quality. In fact, an electric guitar playing power chords can be a very effective pad element in a song, and pads generally like longer reverb decays. On the other hand, many guitar parts sound much more interesting when made to sound larger than life with a very short (.2 or .3 seconds) reverb. Whichever you choose, you'll find that a timed reverb almost always works with just about any kind of guitar.

Exercise Pod - Adding Reverb To The Guitar
E8.12: Follow steps A through I in exercise E8.11.

Adding Reverb To Keyboards

Since there are such a wide variety of keyboards, they each demand their own approach to adding reverb. For instance, since a piano is so percussive, reverbs that are timed to the track usually fit better than reverbs that are not. The exception might be in a solo piano or classical situation, where you're more concerned with putting the piano in or enhancing any ambience already there with an artificial space instead of worrying about how it fits with a rhythm section.

An organ, on the other hand, plays more long sustaining chords, so while it might sound pretty good with a timed reverb, that's not always essential. You usually don't try to make it sound larger than life, so simply putting it in an artificial space works well.

The synthesizer is a hybrid of both, however. It can have all the attack and percussion of a piano or the sustaining pad element of an organ, and anywhere in between. You may want it to sound larger than life, push it back in the mix, or just put it in an artificial space.

Exercise Pod - Adding Reverb To The Piano
E8.13: Follow steps A through I in exercise E8.11, with the addition of the following:

A) Does it sound better if the piano has more reverb and sits further back in the mix, or less reverb and sits in the front?

B) Does it sound better if the reverb is timed or un-timed?

Exercise Pod - Adding Reverb To The Organ
E8.14: Follow steps A through I in exercise E8.11, with the addition of the following:

A) Does it sound better if the organ has more reverb and sits further back in the mix, or less reverb and sits in the front?

B) Does it sound better if the reverb is timed or un-timed?

Exercise Pod - Adding Reverb To Synthesizers
E8.15: Follow steps A through I in exercise E8.11.

Adding Reverb To Strings

Strings sound best when we place them in a medium-to-large artificial hall because that's how we're used to hearing them. Usually this means a Hall or Church setting (if the reverb unit or plug-in has one), with a decay time of two seconds or more. While a short pre-delay of about 10 or 20 ms might allow the attack of the strings to be more noticeable, longer pre-delays don't usually suit any instrument that's a pad element in the mix, like the strings.

Because of the long sustaining quality of the sound of a string section, the decay time is far less important than it is with other instruments.

Exercise Pod - Adding Reverb To The String Section
E8.16: Follow steps A through I in exercise E8.11, with the addition of the following:

A) Does it sound better if the strings have more reverb and sit further back in the mix, or less reverb and sits in the front?

B) Does it sound better if the reverb is timed or un-timed?

C) Does it sound better with longer reverb decay times (beyond 2 seconds)?

Adding Reverb To Horns

We're usually used to hearing a horn (whether it's brass or woodwind) or horn section in a space, but you also might want it further back in the mix, and even occasionally, larger than life. Because most horns have a brisk attack and release, a timed reverb works very well.

Exercise Pod - Adding Reverb To Horns
E8.17: Follow steps A through I in exercise E8.11.

Adding Reverb To Percussion

Just like drums, percussion is made up of short bursts of sound with strong attacks. This means that they benefit greatly from pre-delay and usually like reverbs that are timed to the track. Normally you're not trying to make any of the percussion instruments sound bigger or push them back in the track, you're trying to put them into an environment.

Exercise Pod - Adding Reverb To Bongos And Congas
E8.17: Follow steps A through I in exercise E8.10, but keep in mind that faster decays and pre-delays work best.

Exercise Pod - Adding Reverb To Shakers And Triangles
E8.18: Follow steps A through I in exercise E8.10, but keep in mind that faster decays and pre-delays work best.

Layering The Mix

By now all the vocals and instruments should sound pretty good and everything should be in its own space. Now it's time to tweak the mix.

When layering the mix, we'll be thinking of three things:

1. Are the instruments in front or behind each other in a pleasing manner?

2. Does one of the instruments or vocals need a completely different reverb sound, and therefore its own reverb?

3. Does an instrument or vocal need an effect other than reverb, like a delay or modulation? (We'll cover these in the next two chapters.)

When it comes to layering the mix, we're talking about the reverb balance of each instrument or vocal. Some tracks will be up front and in your face and therefore won't have much reverb on them, or the reverb will be tailored so it isn't obvious using the high- and low-pass filters. Others will have more and more reverb on them and seem to be pushed back in the soundstage as a result. If we were to visually imagine what our mix would be like it would look like Figure 8.7.

Using a combination of different sounding reverbs with different pre-delays and decay times, along with using simply more or less reverb, you can layer the mix like anything the pros might do, because that's how they do it. Keep in mind that each song is unique, so sometimes a a song won't require much reverb or maybe even none at all, but it's all up to you and your ears how you apply what you've learned in this chapter.

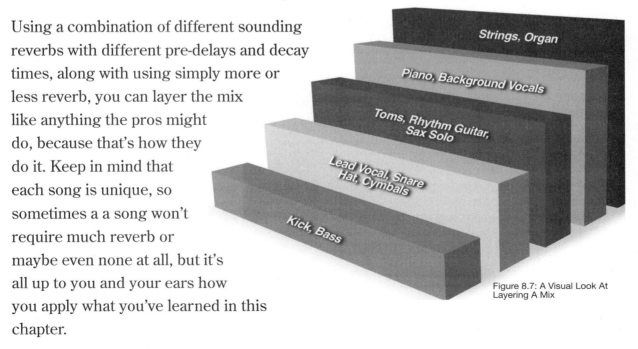

Figure 8.7: A Visual Look At Layering A Mix

Exercise Pod - Layering The Mix

E8.19: Listen to the entire mix with all the reverbs that you've applied so far.

A) Starting from the vocal (or the most important instrument), listen to each track and decide how close to the listener it should sound. Add more reverb if you want to push it back, and less if you want to bring it to the forefront.

B) On the instruments that have the short reverbs, decide how big you want each track to sound. Add more reverb if you want it bigger, and less if you want it smaller. Remember that you may have to adjust the track levels as a result of increasing or decreasing the reverb.

C) If there's an instrument or vocal that still doesn't fit into the mix, try a dedicated reverb with completely different settings from the first two and follow steps A through I of exercise 8.11.

CHAPTER 9
ADDING DELAY

Delay (sometimes called echo) is an integral part of a mixer's toolbox because it's able to make things sound larger than life or push them back in the mix, just like reverb, but does so by being somewhat less noticeable than reverb. In fact, there are some recordings where the only effect is delay and not a speck of reverb is used anywhere, which makes it very powerful.

Delay Basics

Many of the reasons for using delay are the same as with reverb. For instance, delay can be used to:

1. Push a sound back in the mix. By using a longer delay, the track will seem further away from the listener if the level is high enough. Adding more repeats also enhances this effect.

2. Make an instrument or vocal sound larger than life. A very short delay (under 40 milliseconds) reinforces the dry signal while artificially reproducing what's known as the "first reflection" in the room, which is the most powerful and audible part of natural room ambience. Also, by panning the delay to one side of the mix and the dry signal to the other, it widens the sound of the track in the stereo soundstage.

3. Add an artificial double. By adding a 50 to 100 ms delay, you can artificially create the slap-back, double track effect heard on so many of the hits of the 50s (because that's the only effect they had back then).

4. Add a "glue" to the mix. A delay that's timed to the track essentially disappears, but it has the effect of melding the track together in a way that reverb can't do. Veteran mixers call it the "glue" to the mix.

Typical Delay Parameters

There are fewer control parameters than with reverb, but that doesn't make a typical delay any less powerful (see Figure 9.1). They are:

Delay Time: This is similar to decay time in reverb except it's usually measured in milliseconds since it's rare that it's ever as long as a second (which is 1000 milliseconds).

Repeats: The number of repeats (sometimes called Regeneration or Feedback) ranges from 0 to infinity, but most of the time it's set from 0 to 3 repeats or so. Too many repeats makes the mix muddy while too few makes the delay less obvious.

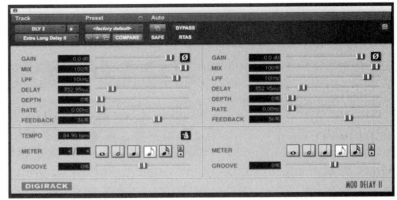

Figure 9.1: Typical Delay Parameter Controls

Filters: Just like reverb, the sound of a delay can be affected greatly by a high-pass and low-pass filter. On most delay plug-ins currently available these are built in, but in many cases you might have to insert them into the effects channel. Just like reverb, inserting a HPF can clean up a mix by eliminating low-frequency information. Eliminating high frequencies with a LPF can make the delay less obvious so that it blends into the track better.

Dry/Wet: The *dry/wet* control (sometimes called mix) allows you to mix the delayed signal with the dry signal. This is essential for dialing in the correct amount of delay if the delay plug-in is inserted on a track, but it's normally set to 100% wet when inserted into a dedicated effects return channel.

Sometimes delay plug-ins also have parameter controls like *Tempo* and *Meter*, which allow the delay to be easily timed to the track.

The Haas Effect

The *Haas Effect* is a very useful psychoacoustic theory that states that a delay of 40 milliseconds or less (depending on which text book you read - sometimes it's noted as 30 milliseconds) is not perceived as a distinct event. That means that if a delay on a snare drum was set to 50 milliseconds, you would hear two separate events - the initial snare hit,

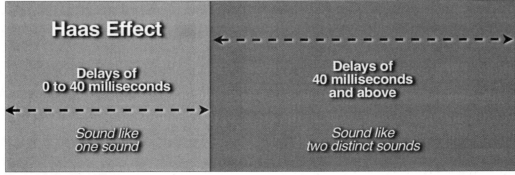

Figure 9.2: The Haas Effect

then the delay. But if you set the delay to less than 30 milliseconds, the two would blend together and you'd hear them both as a single event (see Figure 9.2).

This is important because it means that a short delay of less than 30 milliseconds can be used to thicken a sound that seems a bit thin, or it can be used to "stereoize" a mono track by panning the dry track to one side and the delayed to the other. Regardless how you use it, the Haas Effect is a very powerful, if sometimes overlooked tool in your mixing toolbox.

Timing The Delay To The Track

Just like with reverb, it's important to time your delay to the track unless you want it to be very obvious. The difference is that there are so many more possibilities, depending upon your needs. Timing the delay to the beat of the track can add depth without the delay being noticeable.

Many delay plug-ins allow you to sync to the BPM of the track, which automatically determines the delay times. If this option is not available, you can time the delay to the track by using the following formula:

> 60,000/the beats per minute of the track = delay time in milliseconds

As an example:

> 60,000/125 BPM = 480 milliseconds

This is the delay of a quarter note. If that's too long, you can divide the result of the formula (480 milliseconds) by 2 to get an eighth-note delay of 240 milliseconds. Divide by 2 again and you get a 16th-note delay of 120 milliseconds. You can keep dividing by 2 to get smaller and smaller note divisions.

Another way to time the pre-delay to the track is the use the Ultimate Delay Time iPhone application.

Other Note Divisions

Sometimes the delay sounds better when other note denominations such as triplets or dotted eighths, 16th, etc., are used. These denominations can be determined using the following formula:

> Delay Time x 1.5 = Dotted Value

For example:

> 480 ms (the quarter note 125 BPM delay from the previous example) x 1.5 = 720 ms (Dotted Quarter Note)

> Delay Time x .667 = Triplet Value

For example:

> 480 ms (quarter note 125 BPM delay) x .667 = 320 ms (quarter-note triplet)

As with the straight notes (quarter, eighths, etc.), you can continually divide the above values in half until you get the desired denomination.

While the straight note denominations of quarter, eighth, 16th, and on can provide depth to a track, triplet and dotted note denominations are great for adding glue. They make a track feel good and can blend in seamlessly.

Exercise Pod - Timing The Delay

E9.1: Solo the snare drum and the delay returns (or put them into Solo Safe - refer to your DAW or console manual on how to do this). Be sure that the *Dry/Wet* level is set to 100% wet, and the return levels are set at about -10 on the master bus meter.

A) Find the BPM of the song by using either the tap feature found on most DAWs, or the tap function of a smartphone app like the Ultimate Delay Time.

B) Use the sync feature of the delay or the formula found above (60,000/song BPM) to find the delay time.

C) Set the time for whatever time denomination (16th, 32nd, 64th note) that sets the delay time below 40 ms with no repeats. Does the snare sound bigger? Does it sound more distinct? Does it sound thicker?

D) Un-solo the snare and the reverb returns. Does the snare sound bigger in the track? Does it sound more distinct?

E) Set the repeats for 4. Does it sound better or worse? Does it blend in with the track or does it stick out? Does it make it muddy sounding?

F) What does it sound like if you set the HPF to 250Hz? Does it sit better in the mix?

G) What does it sound like if you set the LPF to 5kHz? Does it sit better in the mix?

H) What does the delay sound like on the lead vocal instead of the snare?

E9.2: A) Solo the snare and delay returns again and set the delay for whatever time denomination (16th, 32nd, 64th note) that sets the delay time between 50 and 100 ms with no repeats. Does the snare sound bigger? Does it sound more distinct? Can you hear the slap? Does it sound thicker?

B) Un-solo the snare and the reverb returns. Does the snare sound bigger in the track? Does it sound more distinct?

C) Set the repeats for 4. Does it sound better or worse? Does it blend in with the track or does it stick out? Does it make it muddy sounding?

D) What does it sound like if you set the HPF to 250Hz? Does it sit better in the mix?

E) What does it sound like if you set the LPF to 5kHz? Does it sit better in the mix?

F) What does the delay sound like on the lead vocal instead of the snare?

E9.3: A) Solo the snare and delay returns again and set the delay for whatever time denomination (1/16th, 1/32nd, 1/64th note) that sets the delay time between 100 and 200 ms with no repeats. Does the snare sound bigger? Does it sound more distinct? Is it more distant? Is it distracting? Does it seem closer or further away from you?

B) Un-solo the snare and the reverb returns. Does the snare sound bigger in the track? Does it sound more distinct? Is it more distant? Is it distracting?

C) Set the repeats for 4. Does it sound better or worse? Does it make it muddy sounding?

D) What does it sound like if you set the HPF to 250Hz? Does it sit better in the mix?

E) What does it sound like if you set the LPF to 5kHz? Does it sit better in the mix?

F) What does the delay sound like with the lead vocal instead of the snare?

E9.4: A) Solo the snare and delay returns again and set the delay for whatever time denomination (16th, 32nd, 64th note) that sets the delay time between 200 and 400 ms with no repeats. Does the snare sound bigger? Does it sound more distinct? Is it more distant? Is it distracting?

B) Un-solo the snare and the reverb returns. Does the snare sound bigger in the track? Does it sound more distinct? Is it more distant? Is it distracting?

C) Set the repeats for 4. Does it sound better or worse? Can you hear the delay?

D) What does it sound like if you set the HPF to 250Hz? Does it sit better in the mix?

E) What does it sound like if you set the LPF to 5kHz? Does it sit better in the mix?

F) What does the delay sound like on the lead vocal instead of the snare?

E9.6: A) Solo the snare and delay returns again and set the delay for a *dotted* time denomination (16th, 32nd, 64th note) that sets the delay time between 200 and 400 ms with no repeats. Does the snare sound bigger? Does it sound more distinct? Is it more distant? Is it distracting? Can you hear the delay?

B) Un-solo the snare and the reverb returns. Does the snare sound bigger in the track? Does it sound more distinct? Is it more distant? Is it distracting?

C) Set the repeats for 4. Does it sound better or worse? Can you hear the delay? Does it sound muddy?

D) What does it sound like if you set the HPF to 250Hz? Does it sit better in the mix?

E) What does it sound like if you set the LPF to 5kHz? Does it sit better in the mix?

F) What does it sound like with the lead vocal instead of the snare?

Delay Setup

Just like with your reverbs, setting up the delays before you begin to mix can save a lot of time and distraction later. Here are a couple of setups to start you off, but eventually you'll develop your own preferences.

The Single-Delay Quick-Setup Method

Designed to get you up and running quickly with a multi-purpose delay that works on just about any kind of track, this quick delay setup can be added to the two-reverb quick setup mentioned in the previous chapter for an instant setup for great sounding rough mixes.

Here's how it works:

Set the delay for a 220 milliseconds delay with a couple of slaps. This delay time is acceptable in most situations on tracks like vocals or guitars. If you want to time the delay to the track, take whatever note denomination comes closest to 220 (like 240 ms in our previous example). Paul McCartney likes his delay a bit lower at 175 ms (which he uses on his voice all the time), but anywhere in that neighborhood will work.

The Three-Delay Full-Setup Method

In this setup we'll use three different delays; one set up for a very short delay, another as a medium and another long (see Figure 9.3). This covers most of the possibilities that might arise during a mix, although it's also possible that one dedicated to a specific mix element (like a solo or lead vocal) might be needed.

> **Delay One:** Set this up for a Haas Effect delay of less than 40 ms and timed to the track with no repeats. It will be used to make a track sound bigger and wider.
>
> **Delay Two:** Set this one up for a short delay of anywhere from 50 to 150 ms with a couple of repeats and timed to the track. This is used for a double or slap delay.
>
> **Delay Three:** Set this for a long delay that will act as your "glue." Shoot for a timed delay that that goes anywhere from 250 to about 400 ms with a couple of repeats. I like to use a triplet or dotted note delay here, but experiment to see what works for the song. If you want the delay to stick out, sometimes a 350-ms, untimed delay works great.

These delay settings are just a starting place will be tweaked as you go along in the mix. Sometimes you may find one of the delay times unnecessary, while other times you may need to add more.

Adding Delay To Instruments

Just like reverb, there's no rule for where and how delay is added to a mix. In some mixes, a single delay can work for every instrument and vocal (just like from all those great hits of 1950s, '60s and '70s when the delay came from a tape machine), while another mix might sound better with a separate delay for every mix element. Here are a few exercises that will allow you to hear each scenario.

Figure 9.3: The Three Delay Setup

Adding Delay To The Vocals

Both lead and background vocals are frequently the primary recipients of some sort of delay in the mix. For a lead vocal, it can provide a sense of space and polish without pushing the vocal too far back in the mix. For the background vocals, it can be a way to distinguish them from the lead vocal.

Exercise Pod - Adding Delay To The Vocals

E9.7: Solo the lead vocal and delay returns again.

A) Raise the level of the send to the Delay #1 with the Haas Effect setting. Does the vocal sound bigger? Is it more distant? Is it distracting? Is it thicker?

B) Un-solo the lead vocal and the reverb returns. Does the lead vocal sound bigger in the track? Is it more distant? Can you hear the delay? Is it distracting?

C) What does it sound like if you lower the delay level until you can just hear it?

D) What does it sound like if you add repeats?

E) What does it sound like if you set the HPF to 250Hz? Does it sit better in the mix?

F) What does it sound like if you set the LPF to 5kHz? Does it sit better in the mix?

G) What does it sound like if you pan the dry vocal to one side and delay to the other?

E9.8: A) Raise the level of the send to the Delay #2 with the slap/double setting. Does the vocal sound bigger? Is it more distant? Is it distracting? Is it thicker?

B) Un-solo the lead vocal and the reverb returns. Does the lead vocal sound bigger in the track? Is it more distant? Can you hear the delay? Is it distracting?

C) What does it sound like if you lower the delay level until you can just hear it?

D) What does it sound like if you add repeats?

E) What does it sound like if you set the HPF to 250Hz? Does it sit better in the mix?

F) What does it sound like if you set the LPF to 5kHz? Does it sit better in the mix?

G) What does it sound like if you pan the dry vocal to one side and delay to the other?

E9.9: A) Raise the level of the send to the Delay #3 with the longer setting. Does the vocal sound bigger? Is it more distant? Can you hear the delay? Is it distracting? Is it thicker?

B) Un-solo the lead vocal and the reverb returns. Does the lead vocal sound bigger in the track? Is it more distant? Is it distracting?

C) What does it sound like if you lower the delay level until you can just hear it?

E) What does it sound like if you set the HPF to 250Hz? Does it sit better in the mix?

F) What does it sound like if you set the LPF to 5kHz? Does it sit better in the mix?

G) What does it sound like if you pan the dry vocal to one side and delay to the other?

Adding Delay To The Guitar

Like the vocal, both acoustic and electric guitars can benefit greatly with a bit of delay. It can make them larger than life, provide a sense of space, or push them back in the mix, depending on what the song requires and what you hear in your head.

Exercise Pod - Adding Delay To The Guitar

E9.9: Repeat exercises E9.7, 9.8 and 9.9 using the guitar instead of the lead vocal.

E9.10: A) For an interesting sound, insert a stereo delay into a guitar channel.

B) Set the left delay for 25 ms, the right for 50 ms, with one or two repeats and the *Dry/Wet* control to taste. Does the guitar sound bigger? Is it pushed back in the mix? Can you hear the delay? Is it thicker?

Adding Delay To Keyboards

All the attributes that a delay brings to a guitar can also be applied to just about any keyboard. While reverb may work better in some situations, never hesitate to experiment with a delay when looking for a sound. The result can be surprising.

Exercise Pod - Adding Delay To Keyboards

E9.11: Repeat exercises E9.7, 9.8 and 9.9 using the piano, organ or synthesizer instead of the lead vocal.

E9.12: A) For an interesting sound, insert a stereo delay into a keyboard channel.

B) Set the left delay for 211 ms, the right for 222 ms, with 2 repeats and the *Dry/Wet* control to taste. Does the keyboard sound bigger? Is it pushed back in the mix? Does it sound like it's in a room? Can you hear the delays?

Adding Delay To The Drum Kit

While delay isn't used as a primary effect on drums very much, it can be used for the glue effect when trying to tie everything in the mix sonically together. If a little bit of the delay that's used on one of the other instruments is added to the snare, it can provide a sense of movement since it can feel like the natural first reflection of a room. This works with toms and even the hi-hat too, although not too well with cymbals.

Exercise Pod - Adding Delay To The Drum Kit

E9.13: A) Raise the send on the snare to Delay #1 with the Haas effect. Does the snare sound bigger? Does it sound smoother? Does it sound like it's in a different space? Does it fit better with the track? Is it thicker?

B) Raise the send on the toms to Delay #1. Do the toms sound bigger? Does it sound smoother? Does it sound like it's in a different space? Does it fit better with the track?

C) Raise the send on the high-hat to Delay #1 with the Haas Effect. Does the high-hat sound bigger? Does it sound smoother? Does it sound like it's in a different space? Does it fit better with the track?

E9.14: A) Raise the send on the snare to Delay #2 with the slap/double effect. Does the snare sound bigger? Does it sound smoother? Does it sound like it's in a different space? Does it fit better with the track? Is it thicker?

B) Raise the send on the toms to Delay #2. Do the toms sound bigger? Does it sound smoother? Does it sound like it's in a different space? Does it fit better with the track?

C) Raise the send on the hi-hat to Delay #2. Does the high-hat sound bigger? Does it sound smoother? Does it sound like it's in a different space? Does it fit better with the track?

E9.15: A) Raise the send on the snare to Delay #3 with the "glue" effect. Does the snare sound bigger? Does it sound smoother? Does it sound like it's in a different space? Does it fit better with the track? Is it thicker?

B) Raise the send on the toms to Delay #3. Do the toms sound bigger? Does it sound smoother? Does it sound like it's in a different space? Does it fit better with the track?

C) Raise the send on the hi-hat to Delay #3. Does the high-hat sound bigger? Does it sound smoother? Does it sound like it's in a different space? Does it fit better with the track?

Adding Delay To Other Instruments

While delay works great on many instruments, there are a few it's rarely used on. You won't hear it much on bass, since it tends to rob the instrument of its power. It's not used much on percussion because it makes the hits sound confusing (although you do hear it on congas every now and again). And you don't hear it much on strings, organ or any other pad element in the mix because the long sustaining notes negate the effect of any delay with repeats.

That being said, don't be afraid to try a delay on any instrument (especially a Haas Effect delay). You just might be surprised what it can do for the sound.

CHAPTER 10
MODULATION EFFECTS

Modulation refers to an external signal that varies the sound of an instrument or vocal in volume, timing or pitch. This includes effects like chorus, flanging and phasing, which are pretty standard mixing tools, to tremolo and vibrato, which are used mostly on guitars and electric pianos.

Between reverb, delay and modulation, modulation is the least used mixing effect because a little goes a long way. And except for flanging, you'll also hear modulation effects used mostly on a single track at a time, instead of across the entire mix. In fact, most modulation effects are inserted directly in the signal path of a channel instead of using a dedicated send and return configuration.

Modulation Basics

While all modulation effects certainly don't sound the same, not many mixers know the difference between them. Let's take a look.

Types Of Modulation

There are three modulation effects that are very closely related; phase shift, chorus, and flange. The simplest difference between them is that a chorus and flange effect comes from a modulated delay that's mixed back into the original signal. The flanger uses a shorter delay than a chorus, usually much less than 5 milliseconds, but a phaser uses no delay at all (see Figure 10.1).

Going a bit deeper, flangers, phasers and choruses work by producing a series of frequency bandwidth notches that are slowly swept across the frequency spectrum of the instrument or vocal. You don't really hear these notches; you hear what's left in the frequency spectrum, which is a series of peaks. Phasers have a small number of notches spaced evenly across the frequency spectrum while flangers and choruses have a larger number that are spaced harmonically.

Tremolo and vibrato work a little differently because no delay is involved. Tremolo cyclically varies the signal up and down in level, while vibrato varies the tone cyclically up and down.

Effect	Delay	Description
Phase Shift	None	Cancels different frequencies to create the effect. Frequency notches spaced evenly across the guitar frequency response.
Flanging	Less than 1ms to 5ms	Deepest depth, has the greatest frequency cancellations. Frequency notches are spaced harmonically across the instrument's frequency response.
Chorus	5 to 25ms	Almost sounds like doubling while widening the sound. Used to thicken the sound and create a stereo image. Frequency notches are spaced harmonically across the instrument's frequency response.
Tremolo	None	Cyclicly changes the volume. Used mostly on guitars.
Vibrato	None	Cyclicly changes the frequency response.

10.1 The Differences Between Modulation Effects

Flangers And Phasers

The flanger is a dramatic effect that was first derived in the '60s by playback of a song on two tape recorders at the same time, and slowing one down by placing your finger on the tape flange, hence the name "flanging." One of the first hit songs that it was used on was a 1967 hit by the British group The Faces called "Itchycoo Park," which featured a large dose of the effect at the end of the song. As these things usually go, once the song became a hit, every artist and producer wanted the effect on their song. The problem was that setting up the two tape recorders needed for the effect was both expensive and very time consuming, so it wasn't long before an electronic simulation of sorts came on the market.

Back in the '70s before the introduction of inexpensive digital delay electronics, an analog phaser was the only way to get any sort of modulated effect, but it was a weak comparison to the intensity of a deep flange, which is why phasing isn't used much — it's just not that dramatic an effect.

Once digital delays came on the market it became possible to simulate true tape flanging, and now just about every modulation plug-in and stomp box does a great job.

Figure 10.2: Boss CE-1 Chorus

Chorus

Chorus differs from flanging in a couple of aspects; the delay needed to achieve the effect is longer, and the frequency notches aren't random like in flanging. You can thank Roland and their Jazz Chorus line of guitar amplifiers introduced in 1980 for starting the chorus craze, which was soon included across their line of keyboards as the world became hooked on the effect. Soon after the amp received such a great response, Roland introduced a version in their Boss line of stompboxes which engineers used to easily add the effect wherever needed during a mix (see Figure 10.2).

Indeed, it's very easy to fall in love with the sound of a chorus because it's lush sounding, and if used in stereo, can really widen the sound of a track quite a bit. If you listen to many hits from the '80s, you'll hear the effect used, used and used some more.

Today, most modulation plug-ins allow you to select between chorus, phasing and flanging, since they're all related.

Tremolo And Vibrato

Tremolo is a cyclic variation in volume, like what you find on Fender amplifiers (even though it's incorrectly labeled as "Vibrato"). Don't confuse tremolo with vibrato because they're different. Vibrato changes the pitch of the sound while tremolo changes the volume.

While tremolo is occasionally used on a guitar or electric piano (both the original Rhodes and Wurlitzer electronic pianos had it built in), vibrato is rarely used since the variation in pitch can make band tuning an issue.

Parameter Settings

The parameters for a phaser, flanger, or chorus, are somewhat the same, which is why all three effects are sometimes combined into the same unit (see Figure 10.3).

Speed/Rate: This control adjusts the speed of the effect. Usually it's set in the low milliseconds from .5 to about 25 cycles per second.

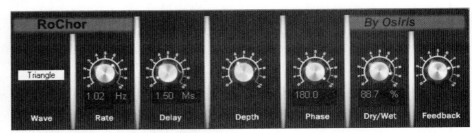

Figure 10.3: Typical Modulation Parameter Controls

Depth/Intensity: Adjusts how much you hear the effect.

Mix: Sometimes a *mix* control, which mixes the wet with the dry signal, is added instead of a *depth* or *intensity* control. In most cases, a mix of 50/50 provides the most intense effect.

Feedback/Regeneration: *Feedback* (sometimes called *regeneration*) takes a little of the output signal of the plug-in or hardware unit and routes it back into the input of the device, which provides an unusual variation to the sound.

Width: This controls how wide the stereo field is.

Delay: On many multi-function modulation devices or plug-ins, the *delay* control is what changes the function from a phaser (no delay) to a flanger (.5 to 5 ms) to a chorus (25 ms) or anywhere in between.

A variety of other controls, from input and output to equalizers and filters, can also be found on some of the more sophisticated devices.

Tremolo/Vibrato

Tremolo and vibrato plug-ins usually have two parameter settings; speed and depth.

Speed: In a tremolo, this control adjusts how fast the volume level will change. In a vibrato, it controls how fast the tuning will change.

Depth: This adjusts the how much of the effect you hear. Sometimes the depth is fixed so this control isn't included.

Modulation Setup

In the 1980s when chorus seemed to be used on nearly everything in a mix, you frequently found a chorus unit patched into its own console returns so it could be easily accessed by a send from any channel. Today we use a chorus only occasionally, and other modulation effects even less, so they're usually patched directly into the signal path of the channel that we want to effect, and the amount used is controlled by the mix or depth control.

On rare occasions, a song may require the entire mix to be flanged at some point, which would require it to be patched into the signal path of the stereo mix bus.

Modulation On Instruments

Unlike reverb and delay, modulated effects are only used consistently on a few instruments. Let's look at those first.

Modulation On Guitars

Distorted electric guitars and modulation seem to fit together like a hand in a glove, although clean electrics and acoustics benefit significantly as well. Want to widen it out in the stereo field? Add a little chorus. What it to sound thicker? Some chorus or a slight flange can help. Want that Eddie Van Halen sound from "Unchained?" That's a flanger he's using.

Tremolo is another go-to effect for guitar that's been used on many hit songs over the years like "Gimme Shelter" by the Rolling Stones, "Born On The Bayou" by Creedence Clearwater Revival, and something a little more current, "The Bends" by Radiohead.

Exercise Pod - Modulation On Guitars

E10.1: Insert a chorus plug-in into a guitar channel (use a hardware unit if you're using a console).

A) Raise the *Rate* control. Does the sound fit the song better? Does it sound better if it's timed to the song? Does it sound better at a slower rate?

B) Raise the *Depth* control. Does the sound fit the song better? Does the sound of the guitar change too much for the song? Are there tuning problems with any other instrument?

E10.2: Insert a flanger plug-in into a guitar channel (use a hardware unit if you're using a console).

A) Raise the *Rate* control. Does the sound fit the song better? Does it sound better if it's timed to the song? Does it sound better at a slower rate?

B) Raise the *Depth* control. Does the sound fit the song better? Does the sound of the guitar change too much for the song? Are there tuning problems with any other instrument?

C) Raise the *Feedback* control. Does the sound fit the song better? Does the sound of the guitar change too much for the song? Are there tuning problems with any other instrument? Does it sound better when the feedback is increased?

D) Raise the *Mix* control. Does the sound of the effect change? Does the sound get smaller or bigger?

E10.3: Insert a tremolo plug-in into a guitar channel (use a hardware unit if you're using a console).

A) Raise the *Rate* control. Does the sound fit the song better? Does it sound better it it's timed to the song? Does it sound better at a slower rate?

B) Raise the *Depth* control. Does the sound fit the song better? Does the sound of the guitar change too much for the song? Are there tuning problems with any other instrument?

Modulation On Keyboards

Chorus or flanging has been used on keyboards almost from the time they were invented. Either can take a boring mono instrument and make it interesting, as well as make it thicker and wider sounding. Be careful not to use too much though (especially on a grand piano), since it not only can change the character of the sound to something dated, but it can cause a tuning problem with other instruments as well.

Tremolo goes very well with electric piano, especially one that cross-pans from the left channel to the right (or vice-versa). The very earliest electric pianos had tremolo built-in, and if you try a little on it, you'll know why.

Exercise Pod - Modulation Of Keyboards

E10.4: Insert a chorus plug-in into a keyboard channel (use a hardware unit if you're using a console).

A) Raise the *Rate* control. Does the sound fit the song better? Does it sound better if it's timed to the song? Does it sound better if the rate is slower?

B) Raise the *Depth* control. Does the sound fit the song better? Does the sound of the keyboard change too much for the song? Are there tuning problems with any other instrument?

E10.5: Insert a flanger plug-in into a keyboard channel (use a hardware unit if you're using a console).

A) Raise the *Rate* control. Does the sound fit the song better? Does it sound better if it's timed to the song? Does it sound better if the rate is slower?

B) Raise the *Depth* control. Does the sound fit the song better? Does the sound of the keyboard change too much for the song? Are there tuning problems with any other instrument?

C) Raise the *Feedback* control. Does the sound fit the song better? Does the sound of the keyboard change too much for the song? Are there tuning problems with any other instrument? Does it sound better or worse if the feedback is increased?

D) Raise the *Mix* control. Does the sound of the effect change? Does the sound get smaller or bigger?

E10.6: Insert a tremolo plug-in into a keyboard channel (use a hardware unit if you're using a console).

A) Raise the *Rate* control. Does the sound fit the song better? Does it sound better if it's timed to the song? Does it sound better if the rate is slower?

B) Raise the *Depth* control. Does the sound fit the song better? Does the sound of the keyboard change too much for the song? Are there tuning problems with any other instrument?

Modulation On Vocals

Sometimes chorus is used on a lead vocal, but in a very subtle way. If a chorus is brought back into the console/DAW on two separate channels besides the vocal, and spread out slightly across the stereo spectrum with the level raised so it's just behind the original vocal, not only will the lead vocal sound bigger, but any tuning inconsistencies can be covered as well.

Chorus or a slight flange on background vocals can also make them sounder thicker and separate them from the lead vocal.

Exercise Pod - Modulation On Lead Vocal

E10.7: Insert a stereo chorus plug-in into two return channels on the DAW (use a hardware unit if you're using a console) and assign a stereo send or a pair of sends to it. Pan the returns all the way to the left and right.

A) On the lead vocal channel, raise the level of the sends to the chorus. What does the vocal sound like? Does it sound better if you lower the return levels?

B) Pan the returns to the 11 and 1 o'clock positions. What does the vocal sound like?

C) Raise the *Rate* control. Does the sound fit the song better? Does it sound better if it's timed to the song? Does it sound better if the rate is slower?

D) Raise the *Depth* control. Does the sound fit the song better? Does the sound of the vocal change too much for the song? Are there tuning problems with any other instrument?

E10.8: Insert a stereo flanger plug-in into two return channels on the DAW (use a hardware unit if you're using a console) and assign a stereo send or a pair of sends to it. Pan the returns all the way to the left and right.

A) On the lead vocal channel, raise the level of the sends to the chorus. What does the vocal sound like? Does it sound better if you lower the return levels?

B) Pan the returns to the 11 and 1 o'clock positions. Does the vocal sound better or worse?

C) Raise the *Rate* control. Does the sound fit the song better? Does it sound better if it's timed to the song? Does it sound better if the rate is slower?

D) Raise the *Depth* control. Does the sound fit the song better? Does the sound of the vocal change too much for the song? Are there tuning problems with any other instrument?

E) Raise the *Feedback* control. Does the sound fit the song better? Does the sound of the lead vocal change too much for the song? Is there tuning problems with any other instrument? Does it sound better or worse if the feedback is increased.

F) Raise the *Mix* control. Does the sound of the effect change? Does the sound get smaller or bigger? Does it sound better with less effect?

Exercise Pod - Modulation On Background Vocals

E10.9: For the background vocals. Insert a stereo chorus plug-in into two return channels on the DAW (use a hardware unit if you're using a console) and assign a stereo send or a pair of sends to it. Pan the returns all the way to the left and right.

A) On the background vocal channels, raise the level of the sends to the chorus. What do the background vocals sound like? Does it sound better if you lower the return levels?

B) Pan the returns to the 11 and 1 o'clock positions. Do the background vocals sound bigger or smaller?

C) Raise the *Rate* control. Does the sound fit the song better? Does it sound better if it's timed to the song? Does it sound better if the rate is slower?

D) Raise the *Depth* control. Does the sound fit the song better? Does the sound of the vocal change too much for the song? Are there tuning problems with any other instrument? Does it sound better with the effect lower in the mix?

E10.10: For the background vocals. Insert a stereo flanger plug-in into two return channels on the DAW (use a hardware unit if you're using a console) and assign a stereo send or a pair of sends to it. Pan the returns all the way to the left and right.

A) On the background vocal channels, raise the level of the sends to the chorus. What does the vocal sound like? Does it sound better if you lower the return levels?

B) Pan the returns to the 11 and 1 O'clock positions. Do the vocals sound bigger or smaller?

C) Raise the *Rate* control. Does the sound fit the song better? Does it sound better if it's timed to the song? Does it sound better if the rate is slower?

D) Raise the *Depth* control. Does the sound fit the song better? Does the sound of the background vocals change too much for the song? Are there tuning problems with any other instrument?

E) Raise the *Feedback* control. Does the sound fit the song better? Does the sound of the background vocals change too much for the song? Are there tuning problems with any other instrument? Does it sound better if the feedback is increased?

F) Raise the *Mix* control. Does the sound of the effect change? Does the sound get smaller or bigger? Does it sound better if the level of the flange is decreased?

Modulation On Strings

Strings and modulation go together like peanut butter and jelly. Sometimes a little chorus on a small string section can make it sound a lot larger than it is, and flanging on strings makes for a very dramatic effect.

Exercise Pod - Modulation On Strings

E10.11: Insert a chorus plug-in into the string channels (use a hardware unit if you're using a console).

A) Raise the *Rate* control. Does the sound fit the song better? Does it sound better if it's timed to the song? Does it sound better if the rate is slower?

B) Raise the *Depth* control. Does the sound fit the song better? Does the sound of the strings change too much for the song? Are there tuning problems with any other instrument? Refer to the string track on Example 2 of the DVD.

E10.12: Insert a flanger plug-in into the strings channel (use a hardware unit if you're using a console).

A) Raise the *Rate* control. Does the sound fit the song better? Does it sound better if it's timed to the song? Does it sound better if the rate is slower?

B) Raise the *Depth* control. Does the sound fit the song better? Does the sound of the keyboard change too much for the song? Are there tuning problems with any other instrument?

C) Raise the *Feedback* control. Does the sound fit the song better? Does the sound of the strings change too much for the song? Are there tuning problems with any other instrument? Does it sound better if the feedback is increased?

D) Raise the *Mix* control. Does the sound of the effect change? Does the sound get smaller or bigger? Does it sound better if the level of the flange is decreased?

Modulation On Other Instruments

There are some instruments that are modulated much less than other instruments. Drums are a good example. Because of the short bursts of energy from a drum hit, most modulation effects aren't that apparent, with the exception of cymbals. Sometimes a bit of chorus can be used to thicken up a snare a bit.

Bass is another instrument that isn't modulated that much, except in those rare instances where it's used as a temporary effect. The reason is that modulation changes the tone of the bass. This can take away the power of the bass sound, which would be detrimental to the song.

Exercise Pod - Modulation On Drums

E10.13: Insert a stereo chorus plug-in into two return channels on the DAW (use a hardware unit if you're using a console) and assign a stereo send or a pair of sends to it. Pan the returns all the way to the left and right.

A) On the snare drum channel, raise the level of the sends to the chorus. What does the snare drum sound like? Does it sound better if you lower the return levels?

B) Pan the returns to the 11 and 1 O'clock positions. What does the snare sound like?

C) Raise the *Rate* control. Does the sound fit the song better? Does it sound better if it's timed to the song? Does it sound better if the rate is slower?

D) Raise the *Depth* control. Does the sound fit the song better? Does the sound of the snare change too much for the song?

E10.14: Insert a stereo flanger plug-in into two return channels on the DAW (use a hardware unit if you're using a console) and assign a stereo send or a pair of sends to it. Pan the returns all the way to the left and right.

A) On the snare channel, raise the level of the sends to the flanger. What do the cymbals sound like? Does it sound better if you lower the return levels?

B) Pan the returns to the 11 and 1 O'clock positions. What does the snare sound like?

C) Raise the *Rate* control. Does the sound fit the song better? Does it sound better if it's timed to the song? Does it sound better if the rate is slower?

D) Raise the *Depth* control. Does the sound fit the song better? Does the sound of the snare change too much for the song?

E) Raise the *Feedback* control. Does the sound fit the song better? Does the sound of the snare change too much for the song?

F) Raise the *Mix* control. Does the sound of the effect change? Does the sound get smaller or bigger?

E10.15: For the cymbals, insert a stereo chorus plug-in into two return channels on the DAW (use a hardware unit if you're using a console) and assign a stereo send or a pair of sends to it. Pan the returns all the way to the left and right.

A) On the cymbal channels, raise the level of the sends to the chorus. What do the cymbals sound like? Does it sound better if you lower the return levels?

B) Pan the returns to the 11 and 1 O'clock positions. Do the cymbals sound better or worse?

C) Raise the *Rate* control. Does the sound fit the song better? Does it sound better if it's timed to the song? Does it sound better if the rate is slower?

D) Raise the *Depth* control. Does the sound fit the song better? Does the sound of the cymbals change too much for the song?

E10.16: Insert a stereo flanger plug-in into two return channels on the DAW (use a hardware unit if you're using a console) and assign a stereo send or a pair of sends to it. Pan the returns all the way to the left and right.

A) On the cymbal channels, raise the level of the sends to the flanger. What do the cymbals sound like? Does it sound better if you lower the return levels?

B) Pan the returns to the 11 and 1 O'clock positions. What do the cymbals sound like?

C) Raise the *Rate* control. Does the sound fit the song better? Does it sound better if it's timed to the song? Does it sound better if the rate is slower?

D) Raise the *Depth* control. Does the sound fit the song better? Does the sound of the cymbals change too much for the song?

E) Raise the *Feedback* control. Does the sound fit the song better? Does the sound of the cymbals change too much for the song?

F) Raise the *Mix* control. Does the sound of the effect change? Does the sound get smaller or bigger?

CHAPTER 11
INTEREST

There's more to mixing than just balancing the instruments and vocals and adding some EQ and effects. To really make a mix rock, it has to both feel good and be interesting as well. How does this happen? By finding the tracks that establish the groove or demand your attention, then emphasizing them.

Developing The Groove

As stated in Chapter 3, the groove is the pulse of the song. While it usually comes from the drums and bass, it could really come from any instrument or even a vocal. And lest you think that the groove is predominantly a fixture of one type of music like funk or R&B, you'll find that a strong groove exists in just about any type of good music, regardless of the genre or style. Don't believe me? Listen to the US Marine Corps band play "Stars And Stripes Forever" and then listen to a typical high school band. The Marines have a groove that makes you want to jump up and march with them just as much as you want to shake your booty to a James Brown or Prince song.

Finding The Groove

The best way to develop the groove is to find the instrument or instruments in the song that supply its pulse. As said before, it's usually the bass and drums, but it could very well be a loop, a keyboard, a guitar, and rarely, a vocal. If a band is playing particularly well together, it may be several instruments at the same time.

Exercise Pod - Finding The Groove

E11.1: Refer to the mix that you've been working on in the previous chapters.

A) Listen to the entire mix all the way through. Is there an instrument (or instruments) that establishes the pulse of the song?

B) If an instrument doesn't stick out as being the pulse of the song, go through each track one by one and raise the level by about 3 dB. After you've listened, return it to its previous level position. Do you hear one or more tracks as establishing the pulse of the song now?

Understand that if you're working on a song that wasn't well performed, there *may not* be a track that establishes the groove. If that's the case, it's usually the producer's call to re-cut the track, or you'll just have to make due with the instrument that feels the best. Remember that mixing is always easier with well recorded tracks, great playing, and excellent arrangements.

Establishing The Groove

Once the instrument (or instruments) that establishes the groove is found, the next step is to emphasize it. This can be done by raising the level as little as 1 dB, or adding an extra bit of compression or EQ to make it stand out a bit more in the mix. Then make sure that the rest of the tracks support your groove instrument by tailoring the mix around it.

Take notice in the exercises below that we're adding very small increments of level, compression or EQ. In theory, 1 dB is the minimum amount that the average person can hear according to most text books (it's actually less than that), and sometimes that's all you need to change the balance or feel in a mix. On just about anything in mixing, always begin with small increments first.

Exercise Pod - Establishing The Groove

E11.2: After your groove tracks are found, try one or more of the following:

A) Raise the level of each of the groove tracks by 1 dB. Can you feel the groove better? If not, add another dB. Can you feel it now? If not, add another dB, but be cautious not to make the tracks too far out in front of the mix.

B) If your groove tracks are already being compressed, add another dB or two of compression. Keep the level the same by adjusting the output control or raising the channel fader. Can you feel the groove better? If the groove tracks aren't compressed, then refer back to Chapter 6 and add compression.

C) If your groove tracks are already equalized, add an additional dB at the EQ points. Can you feel the groove better? If not, add another dB. Can you feel it now? Be cautious that the tracks are not too far out in front of the mix or that they don't clash with another instrument. If you still can't hear the effect, add as much as you feel is necessary.

D) After the groove is established and drives the mix, do any final tweaks to the other tracks to make sure they're not covered up or that they don't clash with the groove tracks.

Emphasizing The Most Important Element

In every song, one mix element is more important than everything else. In dance or electronic music it may be the groove but in a genre like traditional country music it's the vocal. Sometimes it's a riff (like Coldplay's "Clocks") and sometimes it's a loop (like the gang vocal loop that Kanye West uses in "Power"). The job of the mixer is to identify this element and emphasize it in the mix.

Finding The Most Important Element

The most important element of the song is the one that captures your ear and makes you think "Cool!" It could be a modulation or delay effect on an instrument or voice, it could be a unique instrument sound, it could be an interesting hook or riff, or it could be an especially passionate vocal performance. The whole trick is to find that part, then emphasize it.

Exercise Pod - Finding The Most Important Element
E11.3: Refer to the mix that you've been working on in the previous chapters.

A) Listen to the entire mix all the way through. Is there an instrument (or instruments) that captures your ear as unique or interesting? Is there one that's potentially interesting?

B) If an instrument doesn't stick out as being the most interesting in the song, go through each track one by one and raise it by about 3 dB. After you've listened, return it to its previous level position. Do you hear a track that's interesting or potentially interesting now?

Emphasizing The Most Important Element

Once you've found your interesting element, it's time to make sure that it pulls the listener into the song immediately. Like with the groove, this can be done with level, compression, EQ or effects.

Exercise Pod - Emphasizing The Most Important Element
E11.4: After your interesting element is found, try one or more of the following:

A) Raise the level of the track by 1 dB. Does it jump out of the mix more? Does it grab the listener's attention? If not, add another dB. Does it grab your attention now? If not, add another dB, but be cautious that the track isn't too far out in front of the mix.

B) If the selected track is already being compressed, add another dB or two of compression. If you still can't hear the effect, add as much as you feel is necessary. Keep the level the same by readjusting the output control. Does it stand out more in the mix? Does it grab the listener's attention now? If the selected track isn't compressed, then refer back to Chapter 6 and add compression.

C) If your selected track is already equalized, add an additional dB at the EQ points. Does it grab the listener's attention? If not, add another dB. Does it jump out of the mix now? If you still can't hear the effect, add as much as you feel is necessary. Be cautious that the tracks are not too far out in front of the mix or that they don't clash with another instrument.

D) Add 1 dB at 5kHz. Does it grab the listener's attention? If not, add another dB. Does it jump out of the mix now? If you still can't hear the effect, add as much as you feel is necessary.

Making A Mix Element Interesting

In the case of finding a potentially interesting element, you'll have to work a little harder, since it's up to you to take it over the top and make it interesting. This usually takes a lot of experimenting and can take up the bulk of the time during a mix.

Many times radical EQ or rarely used effects like ping-pong delays or a flange with massive regeneration can be just the thing to bring a track to life. You'll never know until you try it with the track.

Exercise Pod - Making An Element Interesting

E11.5: After you've selected an element, try radically EQing the track.

A) Add an LPF to the channel if there's not one already inserted. Gradually lower the frequency. Is there a point where the track becomes more interesting?

B) Add a HPF to the channel if there's not one already inserted. Gradually increase the frequency. Is there a point where the track becomes more interesting?

C) Sweep the midrange of the track with an EQ boosted by 6 dB. Is there a frequency that jumps out? What happens if you boost that frequency even more? What happens if you cut it? Is it more interesting?

D) Add a few dB at 5kHz. Does it grab the listener's attention?

E) Add a few dB at 12kHz. Does it grab the listener's attention?

F) Try a different style of EQ (such as a tube emulation) and repeat steps A through E.

E11.6: After you've selected an element, try radically compressing the track.

A) Increase the Threshold control to where it peaks at about 10 dB of compression. Keep the level the same by readjusting the *Output* control. Does it catch the listener's ear? How about 20 dB?

B) Set the *Ratio* control to 10:1. Keep the level the same by readjusting the *Output* control. Does it catch the listener's ear? How about 20:1?

C) Turn the *Attack* control to as fast as it will go. Does it sound bad or unique? Turn it as slow as it will go. Does it sound bad or unique?

D) Turn the *Release* control to as fast as it will go. Does it sound bad or unique? Turn it as slow as it will go. Does it sound bad or unique?

E) Try a different style of compressor and repeat steps A through D.

E11.7: After you've selected an element, try radically delaying the track.

A) Insert a dedicated delay plug-in into the channel. Adjust the *Mix* control so that you can hear the delay without it being too loud.

B) Time the delay for a quarter-note delay as described in Chapter 9. Is the track now more or less interesting? Does it sound more interesting with more or fewer repeats?

C) Time the delay for a eighth-note delay. Is the track now more or less interesting? Does it sound more interesting with more or fewer repeats?

D) Try other timed note denominations like 16th, 32nd, 64th, etc. Try more or fewer repeats. Is the track now more or less interesting?

E) Does it sound more interesting if the highs or lows are radically filtered out?

F) Try different triplet-note denominations. Is the track now more or less interesting?

G) Try different dotted-note denominations. Is the track now more or less interesting?

H) Try a delay that's not timed to the track set to 350 ms. Is the track more or less interesting? 150 ms? 75 ms?

I) Try a stereo delay and pan the two delays hard left and right. Set the delay times differently on each side (for example an eighth note on the left and a 1/16th note on the right). Is it more interesting?

J) Try a ping-pong delay or any other preset that the delay plug-in may have. Tailor it to the track.

E11.8: After you've selected an element, try adding some radical reverb to the track.

A) Insert a dedicated reverb into the channel. Adjust the *Mix* control so that you can hear the reverb without it being too loud.

B) Set the reverb time as short as it will go. Is the track more interesting?

C) Set the reverb time as long as it will go. Is the track more interesting?

D) Slowly decrease the LPF frequency on the reverb if there is one. Is there a point where it becomes more interesting?

E) Slowly increase the HPF frequency on the reverb if there is one. Is there a point where it becomes more interesting?

F) Increase the pre-delay from 0 to as long as it will go. Is there a point where it becomes more interesting?

G) Try different types of reverbs (hall, chamber, room, plate) and repeat steps A through F. Is there one that's more interesting than the others?

E11.9: After you've selected an element, insert a dedicated chorus into the channel.

A) Adjust the *Mix* control so the effect is very soft to radically loud. Is there a point where it becomes more interesting?

B) Adjust the *Rate* control so the effect is very slow to radically fast. Is there a point where it becomes more interesting?

C) Adjust the *Depth* control so the effect is very soft to radically loud. Is there a point where it becomes more interesting?

D) Adjust the *Feedback* control so the effect goes from 0 to full level. Is there a point where it becomes more interesting?

E) Adjust the *Width* control so the effect goes from wide to narrow. Is there a point where it becomes more interesting?

F) Change the setting to flange (or insert a flanger plug-in), and repeat steps A through E. Does the flange make it more interesting?

G) Change the setting to phaser (or insert a phaser plug-in), and repeat steps A through E. Does the phaser make it more interesting?

Sometimes trying to find the right sound for a track can seem like a never-ending adventure, but keep at it. If nothing works, trying some other plug-ins like guitar simulators or ones that are special effects is the next step. If nothing still seems to work, perhaps no effect was needed in the first place? Perhaps there's a more interesting track to work with?

CHAPTER 12
THE MASTER MIX

While it's easy to pay attention to balancing the mix, adding EQ and effects and everything else that goes along with creating a great mix, the performance of the master mix bus is often overlooked. In this chapter you'll discover how to keep your mix sounding clean, how a bus compressor can make it sound a lot better or a lot worse, and how to know when your mix is finished.

Mixing With Subgroups

In an analog, digital or software console, a circuitry block that performs a function like EQ or panning is called a "stage." A big part of how the mix sounds is the way the master mix bus is driven, or what's known as "gain staging." This means that care is taken so that a stage anywhere in the mixing console isn't overloaded. When this occurs, you may hear distortion even though there's no indication of an overload on the meter or overload indicator. Let's take a look at how to correctly gain stage in order to get the cleanest sound.

As indicated in previous chapters, using subgroups either on your hardware console or your DAW makes it easy to control groups of similar sounding instruments. Having all the drums, all the guitars, and all the background vocals on their own subgroup faders makes it easy to make balance changes quickly. The subgroups do call for proper gain staging for the mix signal to stay clean however, and here's how to do it.

There's a rule of thumb that works on any console, be it analog, digital, or in your DAW—*the subgroup fader levels should always be lower than the master fader level*. That means that if the master fader is set at 0 dB, all the subgroup faders must be set at least -1 dB or more below the master in order to prevent an overload from occurring (see Figure 12.1). If the master fader is set at -10 dB for example, all the subgroup faders must be set below that point in order to avoid an overload of the mix bus (see Figure 12.2).

Just because your subgroups happen to be above the level of the master fader doesn't always mean that you'll get audible distortion, but the tone of the mix might be slightly altered, resulting in a smaller-sounding, less-punchy mix. That's why it's always a good practice to employ the "subgroup below the master" rule.

Exercise Pod - Mixing With Subgroups

E12.1: Use the mix from the previous chapter.

A) Set the *Master Fader* to 0 dB and adjust your mix so the subgroups are lower than the *Master Fader*. Does the mix sound clean? What's happening with the master mix bus meter?

B) Decrease the *Master Fader* to -20 dB and raise the monitor control so that the level you're listening to is as loud as it was before. What does the mix sound like now? Has the tonal quality changed? Can you hear any distortion? What's happening with the master mix bus meter?

The Master Level Meters

The master level meters provide an indication of whether your mix bus level is in a safe zone or the mix bus is distorting. Before we can discuss the proper meter readings a mix should have, let's look at the types of meters that are available.

Figure 12.1: Correct Subgroup Gain Staging

Types Of Meters

There are three types of master mix-bus meters that you'll find on analog and digital consoles and software consoles in a DAW. Sometimes the type of meter is selectable, and in other models or versions, it's fixed.

Figure 12.2: Poor Subgroup Gain Staging

The VU Meter

Everyone knows what a VU meter looks like, but you see fewer and fewer of them on audio gear today (see Figure 12.3) The standard VU (which stands for Volume Units) meter, which was common on all professional audio gear until the late '90s, only shows the average level of a signal and has a response time that's way too slow for use in digital equipment. For instance, when a triangle is recorded it might read -20 dB on a VU meter, but its peaks

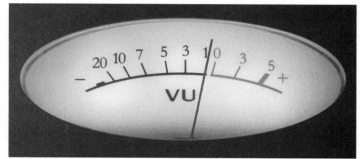

can be as high as +10 dB, which the VU meter (which is sometimes called an "RMS" meter) never indicates. Coupled with the fact that the VU is an analog, mechanical device, and you see why other types of metering is more useful today.

Figure 12.3: A VU Meter

Sometimes a digital meter can be calibrated to respond like a VU meter, but unless it's designed to look like a VU meter, it's called an RMS meter instead. Regardless if it's a hardware or software meter, it's not as useful as other types of metering that are available.

The Peak Meter

The peak meter was created by the British Broadcasting Company when they realized that engineers weren't getting exact enough information from the VU meters they were using. This is especially important in broadcast because if a radio station allows its transmitter to go beyond its assigned transmitter wattage, it will bring a government fine. The problem was that hardware peak meters were expensive to build in the analog world, but they're quite easy in digital. As a result, most digital hardware and software consoles utilize peak meters, which respond rapidly to the signal (see Figure 12.4) and provide a true indication of what the signal is actually doing.

Figure 12.4: A Peak Meter

Unlike VU meters that can read beyond 0 dB, digital peak meters stop at 0, which is known as "full scale" or just FS for short. Any signal beyond that point lights an overload indicator and is considered a digital "over," which creates a very bad sounding distortion that should be avoided at all costs.

Mix Bus Levels

The master fader level should always be kept at a point where the meters never go beyond 0 dB. Although you won't hear immediate distortion on VU/RMS or peak meters, the mix bus on some consoles and DAWs begins to change the sound of the mix from very subtle to quite noticeable as the level goes beyond that point. It's perfectly acceptable to set the Master Fader so the peaks never go beyond -10 dB, and many engineers will routinely do this, especially when mixing "in the box."

By keeping the levels and the meter readings low, it assures plenty of headroom in the signal path so there's never a chance for an internal overload, which can change the sound yet never shows up on the meters.

Many beginning mixers are afraid to set their mix levels low because the level of the song will be low as a result. This isn't much of a worry if your mix will be mastered, since the mastering engineer will boost the level to a commercial level.

Exercise Pod - Setting The Mix-Bus Levels

E12.2: Using the mix from the previous chapter:

A) Set the master fader so that the peaks of the mix go to about -10 dB on the master bus meters. Does the mix sound clean?

B) Set the master fader so that the peaks of the mix go to about 0 dB on the master bus meters. Does the mix sound clean?

C) Set the master fader so that the peaks of the mix go to about +10 dB on the master bus meters. Does the mix still sound clean?

D) Set the master fader back at where the peaks of the mix go to about -10 dB on the master bus meters.

Mix-Bus Compression

Many veteran mix engineers insert a compressor on the stereo mix bus for a number of reasons:

- It raises the level of the mix and gives it more of a finished, mastered sound. Sometimes a client wants to hear what the mix will sound like after mastering, and adding some mix bus compression can simulate the effect.

- It gives the mix a sort of "glue." Many mixers will add only a dB or two of compression just to pull some of the mix elements together in a way that can't be achieved any other way.

Let's take a look at how mix-bus compression is accomplished.

Mix-Bus Compressor Settings

A mix bus compressor is kind of like a bit of fresh ground pepper on a nice salad; a little goes a long way (see Figure 12.5). Most mixers only add 2 or 3 dB of compression on the mix and sometimes even less than that. The reason is that some compressors affect the sound of a mix in a good way without doing much compressing at all.

That being said, in most modern music mix bus compressors are used to make the mix "punchy" and in your face, and the trick to that is to let the attacks through without being affected while the release elongates the sound. Fast attack times reduce the punchiness of a signal, while release times that are too slow make the compressor pump out of time with the music. As mentioned in Chapter 6, the idea is to make the compressor breathe in time with the music.

The bus compressor is typically set at a very low compression ratio of 1.5, 2 to 1 or even 4:1, resulting in only a few dB of compression. The gain is then increased until the song's overall volume level is comparable with the hits of the genre of music you're working in.

Figure 12.5: An SSL Mix Bus Compressor

Here are the steps to set up a bus compressor:

1) Start with the slowest attack and fastest release settings on the compressor.

2) Turn the *Attack* control faster until the high frequencies of the mix begin to dull. Stop at that point, or even back the *Attack* off a touch.

3) Adjust the *Release* control so that the compressor breathes in time with the pulse of the track.

4) Alternately, solo the snare drum and use the method for timing the compression to the track as outlined in Chapter 6.

Exercise Pod - Setting Up the Mix-Bus Compressor

E12.03: Using the mix you worked on in previous chapters, insert a compressor into the mix-bus signal path. Set the compressor to a ratio of 2:1, the attack time as slow as it will go (.5 ms or less if calibrated in milliseconds), and the release time as fast as it will go (200 ms or more if calibrated in milliseconds).

A) Adjust the *Threshold* or Input control until there's 2 dB of gain reduction. What does the mix sound like? Can you hear the compression? Is there any compression indicated on the meter at all?

B) Lower the attack time until the high frequencies begin to dull, then back it off a hair. Adjust the *Threshold* control so there's still only 2 dB of compression. Did anything change in the mix? Can you hear the compression?

C) Raise the release time until you can hear the compressor breathe with the track. If you can't hear it breathe, set it to half-way. Did anything change with the mix? Can you hear the compression? Can you hear any mix element better than before? Is the mix punchier?

D) Set the *Ratio* control to 4:1, but back off the *Threshold* control so that it still reads 2 dB at its peak. Can you hear any difference in the mix?

E) Increase the *Threshold* control until there's 4 dB of compression. Did anything change with the mix? Can you hear the compression? Can you hear any mix element better than before? Is the mix punchier?

F) After the compression is set, raise the Output control on the bus compressor until the peaks reach around -5 dB on the master mix bus meter. Can you hear any difference in the mix?

G) If your mix is going to be mastered, either bypass the bus compressor completely or just add a few dB of compression at most. Any more compression impedes the ability of the mastering engineer to do his job.

E12:4: If you're unable to set the bus compressor by listening to the entire mix, use this method instead. First, insert a compressor into the mix bus signal path. Set the compressor to a ratio of 2:1, the attack time as slow as it will go (.5 ms or less if calibrated in milliseconds), and the release time as fast as it will go (200 ms or more if calibrated in milliseconds). Now try the following:

A) Solo the snare drum. Adjust the *Threshold* control until there's 2 dB of gain reduction. Can you hear the compression? Is there any compression indicated on the meter at all?

B) Lower the attack time until the high frequencies of the snare begin to dull, then back it off a hair. Adjust the *Threshold* control so there's still only 2 dB of compression. Did anything change in the mix? Can you hear the compression?

C) Raise the release time until the level returns to 90 to 100% by the next snare hit. Can you hear the compression?

D) Un-solo the snare. Can you hear the compression in the mix? Can you hear any mix element better than before? Is the mix punchier?

E) Proceed with steps D through G of the previous exercise.

Stay Away From Hypercompression!

Hypercompression is severe over-compression. Although hypercompression seems to be common today, it's very undesirable. It robs the song of life, because there are no dynamics left, and dynamics are a part of what makes music interesting. Radio stations have also proven that hypercompression can lead to listener fatigue, causing listeners to change to a different song in less than a minute (see Figure 12.6). Compression should be used to control dynamics, not eliminate them.

If you're going to have your mix mastered, about the worst thing that you can do is to over-compress it into hypercompression because there's very little for the mastering engineer to work with. In fact, *you're much*

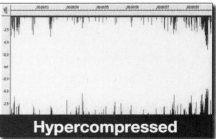

Figure 12.6: A Dynamic Mix Versus A Hypercompressed Mix

better off to provide a mastering engineer with a mix with no bus compression, as that will enable him to fully use his expertise to get you the best final product.

Exercise Pod - The Evils Of Hypercompression

E12.5: Begin with the same setup as in exercise E12.3 and follow steps A through D.

A) Adjust the *Threshold* control until there's 8 dB of gain reduction. Can you hear the compression in the mix? Can you hear any mix element better than before? Is the mix punchier? Are there any dynamics left in the mix? Does it sound better or worse than with only a few dB of compression?

B) Adjust the *Threshold* control until there's 20 dB of gain reduction. Can you hear the compression in the mix? Can you hear any mix element better than before? Is the mix punchier? Are there any dynamics left in the mix? Does it sound better or worse than with only a few dB of compression?

C) Don't hypercompress!

How Long Should My Mix Take?

While many beginning mixers will fly through a mix and be finished in an hour, most mix veterans take a lot longer than that to get a mix together. As you've seen from the previous chapters, a fair amount of experimentation is required to find the parameter settings for EQ, compression and effects that work with the track.

While rough mixes are done very fast by nature (they may only take a couple of passes through the song to get together), and you might occasionally get lucky with a quick mix, most veteran mixers usually figure it takes a 5- to 12-hour day to mix a song. Many mixers like to have an extra half-day to tweak things with a fresh ear, but many big-name, big-budget projects can take weeks of multiple mixes to sculpt it just right.

Of course, if all you have is time, then you can mix a song way beyond its peak (the final mix for Michael Jackson's hit "Billy Jean" was #2 out of 99), so it's best to have a few guidelines as to when it might be finished.

How To Know When Your Mix Is Finished

You can consider a mix finished when the following occur:

- You can feel the groove. Whatever element supplies the groove, it has to be emphasized so that the listener can feel it.

- Every instrument or vocal can be clearly heard. If an instrument or vocal is unintentionally masked or covered by another instrument or vocal, then your mix isn't finished.

- Every lyric and every note of every line or solo must be clearly heard. Each note should be crystal clear. Tweak your fader automation to help this out.

- Be sure the mix is punchy. This is usually a function of the bass and drum EQ and compression.

- The mix has an interesting element. Make sure the most important element of the song is obvious to the listener.

• Be sure your mix sounds good when you play it against other songs that you like. Consider it a job well done when this happens

If time is not a problem, do as many versions as you can until you feel satisfied with your creation. Mixing takes experience so the more time you put in, the better you get at it.

Exercise Pod - Am I Finished Yet?

E12.6: Use the mix that you've been working on in the previous chapters of the book.

A) Listen to the mix. Is the groove obvious? Can you feel it in the mix?

B) Listen to the mix. Can every instrument be clearly heard?

C) Listen to the mix but concentrate on the vocal. Can every lyric be heard?

D) Is the mix punchy?

E) Listen to the mix. What grabs your attention?

F) Play your mix and then play your favorite song. If both songs were played on the radio back to back, would your mix stand up?

CHAPTER 13
THE FINAL MIX

Now that you've made it through boot camp, your ear should be more attuned to what a good mix sounds like, and your mixes should be better than ever. Like so many other things in life, mixing takes practice and the more you do it, the better you get. The more experience you gain, the more you learn what works and what doesn't in a song, and when you hear a sound in your head, you have a better idea of how to go about getting it.

Thanks to the brilliance of modern DAW technology, it's now possible to work on more than one mix at a time. Spend as much time as you need to get your mix sounding as good as it can, but if you run into a roadblock, don't be afraid to put the mix away and work on something else for a while. That's what all veteran mixers do nowadays.

Also keep in mind that there are many roads to the same destination. What I've shown you in this book are some methods that definitely work, but there are others that work too. Don't be afraid to try anything, because you never know when you'll find a technique that fits your style best. Take what works and leave the rest.

Above all, have fun. You can sometimes create magic without it, but everything goes so much easier when everyone is having a good time.

You've now graduated boot camp. Good luck, and go make some great mixes!

GLOSSARY

0 dB Full Scale: The highest level that can be recorded in the digital domain. Recording beyond 0 dB FS results in severe distortion.

Ambience: The background noise of an environment.

Attack: The first part of a sound. On a compressor/limiter, a control that affects how that device will respond to the attack of a sound.

Attenuation: A decrease in level.

Attenuation Pad (sometimes just called a "pad"): A small passive circuit that decreases the input level by a set amount. The pad can be either inline or available as a selection on most preamps. The amount of attenuation is usually in 10dB or 20dB increments.

Automation: A system that memorizes, then plays back the position of all faders, mutes on a console, and just about every parameter in a DAW.

Bandwidth: The number of frequencies that a device will pass before the signal degrades. A human being can supposedly hear from 20Hz to 20kHz so the bandwidth of the human ear is 20 to 20kHz. Sometimes applies to computer Data Rate, where a high rate per second represents a wider bandwidth.

Big Ears: The ability to be very aware of everything going on within the session and with the music. The ability to rapidly dissect a track in terms of key and arrangement.

Bottom: Bass frequencies, the lower end of the audio spectrum. See also "low end"

Bottom End: See bottom.

BPM: Beats per minute. The measure of tempo.

Brick Wall: A limiter employing "look-ahead" technology that is so efficient that the signal will never exceed a certain predetermined level and there will be no digital "overs."

Bus: A signal pathway.

Clean: A signal with no distortion.

Clip: To overload and cause distortion.

Clipping: When an audio signal begins to distort because a circuit in the signal path is overloaded, the top of the waveform becomes "clipped" off and begins to look square instead of rounded. This usually results in some type of distortion, which can be either soft and barely noticeable, or horribly crunchy sounding.

Color: To affect the timbral qualities of a sound.

Comb Filter: A distortion produced by combining an electronic or acoustic signal with a delayed copy of itself. The result is peaks and dips introduced into the frequency response.

Compression: Signal processing that controls and evens out the dynamics of a sound

Compressor: A signal processing device used to compress audio dynamics

Competitive Level: A mix level that is as loud as your competitor's mix.

Cut: To decrease, attenuate or make less.

DAW: A Digital Audio Workstation. A computer loaded with a recording software application that is connected to an input/output interface box.

dB: Stands for decibel, which is a unit of measurement of sound level or loudness. 1 dB is the smallest change in level that a human can hear, according to many textbooks.

Decay: The time it takes for a signal to fall below audibility.

DI: Direct Inject; an impedance matching device for guitar or bass that eliminates the need for a microphone.

Double: To play or sing a track a second time. The inconsistencies between both tracks make the part sound bigger.

Direct: To "go direct" means to bypass a microphone and connect the guitar, bass, or keyboard directly into a recording device.

Direct Box: See DI.

Digital Domain: When a signal source is converted into a series of electronic pulses represented by 1s and 0s, the signal is then in the digital domain.

Digital overs: The point beyond "0" on a digital processor where the red "Over" indicator lights, resulting in a digital overload.

Dynamic Range: A ratio that describes the difference between the loudest and the quietest audio. The higher the number, equaling the greater dynamic range, the better.

Edgy: A sound with an abundance of mid-range frequencies.

Element: A component or ingredient of the mix.

Envelope: The attack, sustain, and release of a sound.

EQ: Equalizer, or to adjust the equalizers (tone controls) to affect the timbral balance of a sound.

Equalizer: A tone control that can vary in sophistication from very simple to very complex (see Parametric Equalizer).

Equalization: Adjustment of the frequency spectrum to even out or alter tonal imbalances.

Feel: The groove of a song and how it feels to play or listen to it.

Flip the phase: Selecting the phase switch on a console, preamp or DAW channel in order to find the setting with the greatest bass response.

Footballs: Musical whole notes. Long sustaining chords.

Fletcher-Munson Curves: A set of measurements that describes how the frequency response of the ear changes at different sound pressure levels. For instance, we generally hear very high and very low frequencies much better as the overall sound pressure level is increased.

Gain: The amount a sound is boosted

Gain Reduction: The amount of compression or limiting.

Gain Staging: Setting the gain of each stage in the signal path so that one stage doesn't overload the next one in line.

Groove: The pulse of the song and how the instruments dynamically breathe with it. Or, the part of a vinyl record that contains the mechanical information that is transferred to electronic info by the stylus.

Haas Effect: A psychoacoustic effect where any delay signal below 40 milliseconds sounds like the same event. In other words, instead of hearing the sound then a delay (two events), you hear both the source and the delay together as a single event.

Headroom: The amount of dynamic range between the normal operating level and the maximum output level, which is usually the onset of clipping.

Hz: An abbreviation for Hertz, which is the measurement unit of audio frequency, meaning the number of cycles per second. High numbers represent high sounds, and low numbers represent low sounds.

High End: The high-frequency response of a device

High-Pass Filter: An electronic device that allows the high frequencies to pass while attenuating the low frequencies. Used to eliminate low frequency artifacts like hum and rumble. The frequency point where it cuts off is usually either switchable or variable.

Hypercompression: Too much bus compression during mixing or limiting during mastering in an effort to make the recording louder results in what's known as Hypercompression, a condition that essentially leaves no dynamics and making the track sound lifeless.

I/O: The Input/Output of a device.

Input Pad: An electronic circuit that attenuates the signal, usually 10 or 20 dB. See also "attenuation pad."

Intermittent: Where the audio cuts in and out or crackles. Guitar cables are frequently intermittent.

In the Box: Doing all of your mixing with the software console in the DAW application on the computer, instead of a hardware console.

Knee: How quickly a compressor will turn on once it reaches the threshold. A "soft knee" turns on gradually and is less audible than a "hard knee."

kHz: 1000 Hertz (example: 4kHz = 4000Hz)

Latency: Latency is a measure of the time it takes (in milliseconds) for your audio signal to pass through your system during the recording process. This delay is caused by the time it takes for your computer to receive, understand, process, and send the signal back to your outputs.

Leakage: Sound from a distant instrument "bleeding" into a mic pointed at another instrument. Acoustic spill from a sound source other than the one intended for pickup.

Limiter: A signal processing device used to constrict or reduce audio dynamics, reducing the loudest peaks in volume.

Look-Ahead: In a mastering limiter, look-ahead processing delays the audio signal a small amount (about 2 milliseconds or so) so that the limiter can anticipate the peaks in such a way that it catches the peak before it gets by.

Low-Pass Filter (LPF): An electronic frequency filter that allows only the low frequencies to pass while attenuating the high frequencies. The frequency point where it cuts off is usually either switchable or variable.

Low End: The lower end of the audio spectrum, or bass frequencies usually below 200Hz.

Make-up Gain: A control on a compressor/limiter that applies additional gain to the signal. This is required since the signal is automatically decreased when the compressor is working. Make-up Gain "makes up" the gain and brings it back to where it was prior to being compressed.

Mastering: The process of turning a collection of songs into a record by making them sound like they belong together in tone, volume, and timing (spacing between songs).

Metadata: Data that describes the primary data. For instance, metadata can be data about an audio file that indicates the date recorded, sample rate, resolution, etc.

Midrange: Middle frequencies starting from around 250Hz up to 4000Hz.

Mix Bus: The network that mixes all of the individual channels together for your final mix.

Modeling: Developing a software algorithm that is an electronic representation of the sound of hardware audio device down to the smallest behaviors and nuances.

Modulation: Using a second signal to modify the first. A chorus uses a very low-frequency signal to modulate the audio signal and produce the effect.

Mono: Short for monaural, or single audio playback channel.

Monaural: A mix that contains a single channel and usually comes from only a one speaker.

MP3: The de facto standard data compression format used to make audio files smaller in size.

Muddy: Non-distinct because of excessive low frequencies.

Multi-Band Compression: A compressor that is able to individually compress different frequency bands as a means of having more control over the compression process.

Mute: An On/Off switch. To mute something would mean to turn it off.

Overs: Digital Overs occur when the level is so high that it tries to go beyond 0 dB Full Scale on a typical digital level meter found in just about all equipment. A red Overload indicator usually will turn on, accompanied by a the crunchy, distorted sound of waveform clipping.

Out of Phase: The polarity of two channels (it could be the left and right channel of a stereo program) are reversed, thereby causing the center of the program (like the vocal) to diminish in level. Electronically, when one cable is wired backwards from all the others.

Pan: Short for panorama - indicates the left and right position of an instrument within the stereo spectrum.

Panning: Moving a sound across the stereo spectrum.

Parametric Equalizer: A tone control where the gain, frequency and bandwidth are all variable.

Peaks: A sound that's temporarily much higher than the sound surrounding it.

Phantom Image: In a stereo system, if the signal is of equal strength in the left and right channels, the resultant sound appears to come from in between them. This is a phantom image.

Phase: The relationship between two separate sound signals when combined into one.

Phase Shift: The process during which some frequencies (usually those below 100Hz) are slowed down ever so slightly as they pass through a device. This is usually exaggerated by excessive use of equalization and is highly undesirable.

Phase Meter: A dedicated meter that displays the relative phase of a stereo signal.

Plug-In: An add-on to a computer application that adds functionality to it. EQ, modulation and reverb are examples of DAW plug-ins.

Point: The frequencies between 2k and 5kHz that cause a sound to be more distinct.

Power Chords: long sustaining, distorted guitar chords.

Pre-Delay: The time between the dry sound and the onset of reverberation. The correct setting of the pre-delay parameter can make a difference in the clarity of the mix.

Presence: Accentuated upper midrange frequencies (anywhere from 5 to 10kHz)

Producer: The equivalent of a movie director, the producer has the ability to craft the songs of an artist or band technically, sonically and musically.

Proximity Effect: The inherent low-frequency boost that occurs with a directional microphone as it gets closer to the signal source.

Punchy: A description for a quality of sound that infers good reproduction of dynamics with a strong impact. The term sometimes means emphasis in the 200Hz and 5kHz areas.

Pumping: When the level of a mix increases, then decreases noticeably. Pumping is caused by the improper setting of the attack and release times on a compressor.

Q: The bandwidth, or the frequency range of a filter or equalizer.

Ratio: A parameter control on a compressor/limiter that determines how much compression or limiting will occur when the signal exceeds the threshold.

Record: A generic term for the distribution method of a recording. Regardless of whether it's a CD, vinyl, or a digital file, it is still known as a record.

Release: The last part of a sound. On a compressor/limiter, a control that affects how that device will respond to the release of a sound.

Resonance: see Resonant Frequency

Resonant Frequency: A particular frequency or band of frequencies that are accentuated, usually due to some extraneous acoustic, electronic, or mechanical factor.

Return: Inputs on a recording console especially dedicated for effects devices such as reverbs and delays. The Return inputs are usually not as sophisticated as normal channel inputs on a console.

RMS Meter: A meter that reads the average level of a signal.

Roll Off: To attenuate either end of the frequency spectrum.

Shelving Curve: A type of equalizer circuit used to boost or cut a signal above or below a specified frequency. Usually the high- and low-band equalizers built into many mixing boards are the shelving type.

Sibilance: A short burst of high-frequencies in a vocal due to heavy compression, resulting in the "S" sounds being over-emphasised.

Signal Path: The electronic or digital circuitry that the signal must pass through.

Soundfield: The direct listening area.

Source: An original master that is not a copy or a clone.

Spectrum: The complete audible range of audio signals.

SPL: Sound Pressure Level.

Stage: In an analog console, a block of circuitry that performs a console function, like EQ or panning. In a digital or software console, a digital block that performs a console function.

Standing Waves: An acoustic property of a room where certain frequencies reflect off the walls that will either boost the signal or attenuate it depending upon where in the room you're standing.

Sympathetic Vibration: vibrations, buzzes and rattles or notes that occur in areas of an instrument, or other instruments, other than the one that was struck.

Subgroup: A separate sub-mixer within a hardware or software console that sums the assigned channels together, then sends that mix to the master mix bus.

Tempo: The rate of speed that a song is played.

Threshold: The point at which an effect takes place. On a compressor/limiter for instance, the threshold control adjusts the point at which compression will begin.

Timbre: Tonal color.

Trim: A control that sets the gain of a device, or the process of reducing the size or playing time of an audio file.

Track: A term sometimes used to mean a song. In recording, a separate musical performance that is recorded.

Top End: See High End.

Transient: A very short duration signal.

Tremolo: A cyclic variation in volume.

Transformer: An electronic component that either matches or changes the impedance. Transformers are large, heavy and expensive but are in part responsible for the desirable sound in vintage audio gear.

Tube: Short for vacuum tube; an electronic component used as the primary amplification device in most vintage audio gear. Equipment utilizing vacuum tubes run hot, are heavy, and have a short life, but have a desirable sound.

Unity Gain: When the output level of a process or processor exactly matches its input level.

Vibrato: A cyclic variation in tone.

WAVE: A WAVE file is an audio data file developed by the IBM and Microsoft corporations, and is the PC equivalent of an AIFF file. It is identified by the ".wav" file extension.

BIBLIOGRAPHY

The Mixing Engineer's Handbook 2nd Edition (ISBN #1598632515 - Thomson Course Technology) - The premier book on audio mixing techniques provides all the information needed to take your mixing skills to the next level along with advice from the world's best mixing engineers.

The Recording Engineer's Handbook 2nd Edition (159863867X - Course Technology PTR) - Revealing the microphone and recording techniques used by some of the most renowned recording engineers, you'll find everything you need to know to lay down great tracks in any recording situation, in any musical genre, and in any studio.

The Audio Mastering Handbook 2nd Edition (ISBN #1598634496 - Course Technology PTR) - Everything you always wanted to know about mastering, from doing it yourself to using a major facility, utilizing insights from the world's top mastering engineers.

The Drum Recording Handbook with DVD (with Dennis Moody) (ISBN #1423443438 - Hal Leonard) - Uncovers the secret of amazing drum recordings in your recording studio even with the most inexpensive gear. It's all in the technique, and this book/DVD will show you how.

How To Make Your Band Sound Great with DVD (ISBN #1423441907 - Hal Leonard) - This band improvement book and DVD shows your band how to play to its fullest potential. It doesn't matter what kind of music you play, what your skill level is, or if you play covers or your own music, this book will make you tight, it will make you more dynamic, it will improve your show and it will improve your recordings.

The Studio Musician's Handbook with DVD (with Paul ILL) (ISBN #1423463412 Hal Leonard) - Everything you wanted to know about the world of the studio musician including how you become a studio musician, who hires you and how much you get paid, what kind of skills you need and what gear you must have, the proper session etiquette required to make a session run smoothly, and how to apply these skills in every type of recording session regardless if it's in your home studio or Abbey Road.

Music 3.0 - A Survival Guide To Making Music In The Internet Age (ISBN #1423474015 Hal Leonard) - The paradigm has shifted and everything you knew about the music business has completely changed. Who are the new players in the music business? Why are traditional record labels, television, and radio no longer factors in an artist's success? How do you market and distribute your music in the new music world - and how do you make money? This book answers these questions and more in its comprehensive look at the new music business - Music 3.0.

The Music Producer's Handbook (ISBN 978-1423474005 Hal Leonard) - Reveals the inside information and secrets to becoming a music producer and producing just about any kind of project in any genre of music. Among the topics covered is the producer's responsibilities, and all the elements of a typical production including budgeting, contracts, selecting the studio and engineer, hiring session musicians, and even getting paid! The book also covers the true mechanics of production, from analyzing and fixing the format of a song, to troubleshooting a song when it just doesn't sound right, to getting the best performance and sound out of the band and vocalist.

The Musician's Video Handbook (ISBN 978-1423484448 Hal Leonard) - Describes how the average musician can easily make any of the various types of videos now required by a musical artist either for promotion or final product. But just shooting a video isn't enough. The book will also demonstrate the tricks and tips used by the pros to make it look professionally done, even with inexpensive gear and not much of a budget.

Mixing And Mastering With T-Racks: The Official Guide (ISBN 978-1435457591 Course Technology PTR) -T-RackS is a popular stand-alone audio mastering application that includes a suite of powerful analog-modeled and digital dynamics and EQ processor modules that also work perfectly as plug-ins during mixing. While T-RackS is an extremely powerful tool for improving the quality of your recordings, all of that power won't do you much good if it's misused. With *Mixing and Mastering with IK Multimedia T-RackS: The Official Guide*, you can learn how to harness the potential of T-RackS and learn the tips and tricks of using T-Racks processor modules to help bring your mixes to life, then master them so they're competitive with any major label release.

The Touring Musician's Handbook (ISBN 978-1423492368 Hal Leonard) - For a musician, touring is the brass ring. It's the thing that everyone dreams about from the first time

they pick up an instrument. But what do you do when you finally get that chance? How do you audition? What kind of chops do you need? What equipment should you bring? How do you prepare for life on the road? Regardless of whether you're a sideman, solo performer, or member of a band, all of these questions are answered in *The Touring Musician's Handbook*. As a bonus, individual touring musician guides for guitar, bass, drums, vocals, keys, horns and strings as well as interviews with famous and influential touring players are also included.

The Ultimate Guitar Tone Handbook (ISBN 978-0739075357 Alfred Music Publishing) - *The Ultimate Guitar Tone Handbook* is the definitive book for discovering that great guitar sound and making sure it records well. The book definitively outlines all the factors that make electric and acoustic guitars, and amplifiers and speaker cabinets sound the way they do, as well as the classic and modern recording and production techniques that capture great tone. *The Ultimate Guitar Tone Handbook* also features a series of interviews with expert players, technicians, recording engineers, producers and manufacturers that gives you an inside look into the business of guitar tone, and an accompanying DVD provides both an audio and visual reference point for achieving the classic sounds you hear on records.

The Studio Builder's Handbook (ISBN - 978-0739077030 Alfred Music Publishing) - No matter how good your recording gear is, chances are you're not getting the best possible sound because of the deficiencies of your room. While you might think that it costs thousands of dollars and the services of an acoustic designer to improve your studio, *The Studio Builder's Handbook* will strip away the mystery of what makes a great sounding studio and show how you can make a huge difference in your room for as little as $150.

You can get more info and read excerpts from each book by visiting bobbyowsinski.com.

Bobby Owsinski's Social Media Connections

Bobby's Music Production Blog - bobbyowsinski.blogspot.com

Bobby's Music Industry Blog - music3point0.blogspot.com

Bobby On Facebook - facebook.com/bobbyowsinski

Bobby On Twitter - @bobbyowsinski

Bobby On YouTube - youtube.com/polymedia

INDEX